Web 2.0 and Libraries:
Impacts, technologies and trends

CHANDOS
INFORMATION PROFESSIONAL SERIES

Series Editor: Ruth Rikowski
(email: Rikowskigr@aol.com)

Chandos' new series of books are aimed at the busy information professional. They have been specially commissioned to provide the reader with an authoritative view of current thinking. They are designed to provide easy-to-read and (most importantly) practical coverage of topics that are of interest to librarians and other information professionals. If you would like a full listing of current and forthcoming titles, please visit our web site www.chandospublishing.com or email info@chandospublishing.com or telephone +44 (0) 1223 891358.

New authors: we are always pleased to receive ideas for new titles; if you would like to write a book for Chandos, please contact Dr Glyn Jones on email gjones@chandospublishing.com or telephone number +44 (0) 1993 848726.

Bulk orders: some organisations buy a number of copies of our books. If you are interested in doing this, we would be pleased to discuss a discount. Please contact Hannah Grace-Williams on email info@chandospublishing.com or telephone +44 (0) 1223 891358.

Web 2.0 and Libraries: Impacts, technologies and trends

EDITED BY
DAVE PARKES
AND
GEOFF WALTON

Chandos Publishing
Oxford · Cambridge · New Delhi

Chandos Publishing
TBAC Business Centre
Avenue 4
Station Lane
Witney
Oxford OX28 4BN
UK
Tel: +44 (0) 1993 848726
Email: info@chandospublishing.com
www.chandospublishing.com

Chandos Publishing is an imprint of Woodhead Publishing Limited

Woodhead Publishing Limited
Abington Hall
Granta Park
Great Abington
Cambridge CB21 6AH
UK
www.woodheadpublishing.com

First published in 2010

ISBN:
978 1 84334 346 2

© The editors and contributors, 2010

Typeset by Domex e-Data Pvt. Ltd.
Printed in the UK and USA.
Printed in the UK by 4edge Limited – www.4edge.co.uk

Contents

PART 2 PEOPLE

List of figures

Preface

In the last five years there has been a phenomenal growth in the widespread adoption of the term Web 2.0 (originally coined in 1999), and the use of its associated emerging technologies. Web 2.0 is a controversial, all-embracing term, used as shorthand for anything from RSS, social networking, blogs, wikis, collaborative and open source software, video and image sharing, web services and folksonomies, to a host of other tools and applications.

Most would agree that whatever Web 2.0 is, it is in a state of 'constant beta', and with this in mind we suggest that this book be regarded as a narrative describing experience so far and a signpost to further developments, rather than a definitive work. Web 2.0 is not just about technology, of course, and that is why this work explores its effect on people, especially the social aspects of working and learning together. It looks too at place, real and virtual, and gives an extensive overview of technologies and software.

The authors are experts in their field and they look at aspects of Web 2.0 through the lens of their extensive knowledge. They are drawn from a range of professions, from information scientists to learning technologists, and their combined view gives a rich picture of how Web 2.0 is affecting the world of work and education. If there is one message to take away from the thoughts put forward here it is that we the educators, technologists or information professionals should regard the transformative change potential of the Web 2.0 landscape as a real opportunity imbued with endless possibility.

Acknowledgements

Dave Parkes

The innovations in emerging technologies we have witnessed over the last few years have started to challenge almost all of my assumptions of what a library can be – not in the technology itself but the engine of community involvement it has generated. Customers can be partners, authors, co-creators of the vision of a library – a library that is always open, always on, physical and virtual, static and mobile, morphing and changing to meet future needs and expectations. A library is a mixed economy of open source, managed service and hand-built solutions – they don't stand alone any longer, they are connected entities.

I am delighted to say that the librarians and learning technologists delivering this vision at Staffordshire University are incredible, innovative and driven individuals. I would like to acknowledge and thank them for being a delight to work with and a source of inspiration.

I also thank Geoff my companion editor for continual encouragement and harassment over deadlines – this book would not exist without his tenacity.

My children Jack and Izzie are a source of wonder and delight. I watch them learn and use technology with what appears to be an innate confidence and consummate skill, and they still have the patience to explain to me what it is they are doing.

I would like to thank my wife Carol for putting up with the conversations held over the screen of the laptop during the gestation of this book – for being an inspiration... and for everything.

Geoff Walton

My interests in Web 2.0 emerged from two very distinct areas: first, research I carried out as part of my PhD at Loughborough University under the guidance of Mark Hepworth; and second, conversations with Dave in meetings, conferences, on the train, in corridors and when fighting over the printer! Through my PhD research it became clear very early on that harnessing the social aspects of learning and then transferring them to the virtual domain provides a very rich and powerful learning experience. My work focused on the nexus of four domains: learning, e-learning, information literacy and information behaviour. Using the scholarship from these domains provided the foundation for a successful online social network learning intervention. Given the rapid changes in Web 2.0 it seemed to me that we need to devise learning structures and ways of working which transcend the shape shifting technologies that make up Web 2.0. This book goes some way to addressing that issue. Conversations with Dave have shown me that we are on the cusp of a real revolution, especially in the way information is presented, disseminated and used.

I would like to thank all of the contributors for their erudite and expert chapters. I enjoyed reading their work, which led me on many interesting journeys of discovery. I would also like to thank my colleagues for their encouragement and support while I carried out my research and teaching: Jamie Barker, Jamie Cleland, Shaun Coates, Andrea Hatton, Paul Johnson, Kathleen Morgan, Alison Pope and Deb Roberts. Special thanks to Joanne Walton at the City of Sunderland College for carrying out the study with A-level sociology students mentioned in Chapter 3. I must not forget to mention my daughters Kath and Hannah. Finally, and most important of all, I would like to thank my wife Caroline for listening, encouraging me and supporting me in my work.

We would like to thank Tim O'Reilly for giving us permission to reproduce his Web 2.0 meme map.

We would also like to thank all those at Chandos, especially Susannah Wight, who have supported this venture to its completion.

Contributors' biographies

Liz Hart

Previously Director of Information Services at Staffordshire University, Liz now operates as a consultant within Liz Hart Associates.

Dr Mark Hepworth

Dr Mark Hepworth is a senior lecturer at Loughborough University in the Department of Information Science. Before that he worked for Nanyang Technological University in Singapore. He teaches information literacy, information retrieval and the development of user-centred information services. His research concerns understanding learners and their interaction with information and as a result he has worked with people in a range of contexts, in the UK and overseas, including management consultants, corporate financiers, informal carers, students, librarians, people with multiple sclerosis – either to help develop systems that support their learning or to help them develop an approach, skills and knowledge to learn independently. He is curriculum adviser for the national CILIP (Chartered Institute of Library and Information Professionals) committee on information literacy.

Brian Kelly

Brian works at UKOLN, a national centre of expertise in digital information management, which is based at the University of Bath. Brian became involved in the web in its infancy, when he helped set up a website in January 1993 while working at the University of Leeds. He moved to his current job in 1996. Brian is an experienced speaker, having given over 300 presentations during his time at UKOLN. Brian was presented with the Information World Review's Information Professional of the Year award at the Inline Information 2007 conference. Brian's current interests include making use of standards and supporting accessibility from a user-focused position, exploring the potential of Web 2.0 and developing best practices for individual and organisational use of Web 2.0. His recent publications include *Time To Stop Doing and Start Thinking: a framework for exploiting Web 2.0 services*, *Contextual Web Accessibility: maximizing the benefit of accessibility guidelines* and *A Contextual Framework for Standards*.

David Ley

David is Project Manager for Technology Research and Delivery at Becta and writes and talks widely about the possibility and application of emerging technologies in education. Becta ensures the efficient and effective use of technology in influencing strategic direction and the development of national education policy. The agency works mainly with government departments within the Department for Children, Schools and Families (DCSF) and the Department for Business, Innovation and Skills (BIS).

Dave Parkes

David is Associate Director of Information Services at Staffordshire. A librarian by trade, David leads a dynamic learning support team of librarians, educational technologists, trainers, IT professionals, study skills staff and web designers to provide a broad array of quality services, resources and learning opportunities. A Fellow of the Higher Education Academy, he writes and speaks widely on the provision of information and digital literacy, e-books and emerging technologies to universities, publishers, academics and other librarians. He sits on the Horizon Report Project board for 2010, and a number of publisher advisory boards. He has recently undertaken consultancy for the Oxford University Russia Fund to help develop e-book provision in Russian universities. He is also Head of the Special Collections and Archives and chairs Inspire West Midlands – the co-operative cross-sectoral access scheme involving all NHS, higher and further education, public and special libraries in the region.

Helen Walmsley

Helen is E-learning Models Co-ordinator at Staffordshire University. This role involves her identifying best practice models for e-learning based on theory and practice and presenting them to teachers to help them develop their practice. Helen manages an online community of practice and collaboration network with over 600 members.

Dr Geoff Walton

Geoff Walton is Academic Skills Tutor Librarian and Research informed Teaching (RiT) Project Co-ordinator at

Staffordshire University. His specific subject responsibilities are for psychology and sport and exercise science. As RiT Co-ordinator Geoff is involved in identifying synergies between research, teaching, learning, information literacy, e-learning and inquiry-based learning. He recently completed a PhD which analysed the development of a blended approach (a mix of face-to-face and online pedagogical methods) for delivering information literacy to first year undergraduates. He is particularly interested in the cognitive processes involved in becoming information literate. His research interests also include developing the Assignment Survival Kit (ASK), developing a process for online peer assessment and investigating academic skills needs in undergraduate students. Geoff is information literacy training officer for the CILIP Community Services Group Information Literacy sub-group.

Dr Jenny Yorke

Jenny is the Learning Development Coordination Manager for Learning Development and Innovation at Staffordshire University and is responsible for strategy for the quality enhancement of e-learning, including e-learning models and the evaluation of e-learning.

Part 1:
Place

The changing teaching and learning environment

Mark Hepworth

In higher education (HE) and further education (FE) a plethora of debate, discussion and advice about how to teach, the 'new' learner and the new technologies available for teaching bombards educators and researchers and filters out into the public domain. This is delivered via the usual channels: conferences, articles and books, websites, discussion lists, blogs, videos and other evolving media. The speed of change and the quantity of both good and poor information is daunting. This introduction attempts to tease out some of the factors driving these changes and to set the scene for the chapters that follow. The latter explore in more depth the experience of people implementing and managing the new learning environments.

In particular this chapter seeks to answer two questions:

- Do the changes that have taken place reflect a reprioritisation of norms and values or are they something fundamentally new?
- Are the new technologies driving change or enabling us to do what we already know should be done?

This discussion is structured under four headings: the cultural and social context, the learner, the teacher and teaching interventions, and tools and technologies.

The cultural and social context is explored in more depth by Dave Parkes in Chapter 2; the learner by Geoff Walton in Chapter 3; teaching interventions again in Chapter 3; the teacher by Jenny Yorke and Helen Walmsley in Chapter 4; and finally tools and technologies are explored by Brian Kelly in Chapter 5 and David Ley in Chapter 6.

The cultural and social context

Over the last 20 years we have seen greater value being placed on human capital – skills and knowledge and the commodification of information (World Bank, 2007) – and the services that facilitate access to information in both domestic and organisational domains (Hepworth, 2007), whether they identify the 'best buy' or are sophisticated corporate or scientific data-mining solutions.

This has been accompanied by a desire by governments and employers for all people, rather than a select minority, to have what has been termed key transferable skills, and phrases such as information literacy, digital literacy and media literacy have become commonplace (Hepworth and Walton, 2009). Such key skills include the ability:

- to develop information and knowledge management strategies
- to understand information needs
- to develop critical and creative thinking including the ability to analyse, evaluate and synthesise information and data
- to organise and manage information
- to be effective at seeking, communicating and sharing data, information and knowledge whether face-to-face or via text, numbers and images electronically or using other media, including networking and collaborating

- to be aware of the etiquette and ethical issues that surround these processes
- to be able to motivate oneself, manage time and continuously learn independently.

These skills are recognised as important for individuals, furthering personal empowerment and enhancing a person's quality of life, and for members of organisations or society at large.

There is no longer a small number of highly disciplined learners who are used to and willing to accept relatively dull forms of learning delivery, or people who seek out information and intellectual stimulus independently, or even produce information and knowledge as part of their being well-rounded, fulfilled, individuals. There are no longer people who were destined for a small number of professional roles and the higher echelons of society, who consumed and produced relatively scarce information products and services.

Independent learning norms and the value previously placed on them for the few is, as implied above, not new. However, these norms have become an expectation for a larger proportion of people in our society and this to some extent may explain the decision by governments in the developed world to encourage all young people to aim for a place in FE or HE. This in turn has led to changes in the educational environment where the number of students has exploded and students come from a greater range of socio-economic backgrounds than in the past.

This has also been associated with an exponential growth in the number of technologies that enable the production, organisation and dissemination of information – formal and informal – commonly linked with concepts such as 'information overload', 'self-publishing' and 'social media'.

The learner

Numerous terms have been used to describe the 'new' learners – 'the Google generation', 'digital natives', 'the Y generation', 'millennials' – as if they were a completely new phenomenon. The 'new' learners have been characterised (Howe and Strauss, 2000; Prensky, 2001; Windham, 2005) as being pragmatic (only doing what is necessary to achieve reward or concrete outcomes); unable to concentrate for long periods of time; wanting an active learning environment where they can access learning when they want, in a form they want (brief, colourful, with little text, to the point, using multimedia); multitasking; and expecting learning to be entertaining. Learners seem to be highly gregarious, enjoying social interaction and being part of a social cohort. The latter may not have changed. However, the consumer society with its attendant expertise at branding and marketing may mean that this feeling of alliance with a group – a reflection of the need for market segmentation, and the associated transient commodities and technologies, such as the MySpace or the Nintendo generation – has been enhanced.

In contrast learners are expected to be highly motivated and independent, and to have the key skills identified above. Educators are often frustrated by this contradiction between society's expectations and the apparent characteristics of the 'new' learner, but I would argue that the characteristics of learners have not changed. Most people, whatever their age or background, get bored and lose attention after 20 minutes of listening to a speaker who uses the old-fashioned lecturing style that many of us older folk were used to in our school and university days. It has long been recognised that people use the method that requires least effort from them when they seek information. However, we knew no different and had no choice. Nowadays people can choose how they learn and are presented with information and learning in a variety of forms and media – video, animation, music, printed text, web text, chat and so on, via phones, the internet, television, theatre or magazines. The professions associated with information dissemination, including school teachers, have also honed their art, drawing on the long history of communication and using the expanding range of media, hence raising expectations.

This has meant that learners are perceived and perceive themselves as consumers of education, particularly in HE where they now have to pay tuition fees. They have high expectations about information provision and the learning environment. This includes expecting the learning experience to meet their needs, wants and desires, and being less used to adapting passively to a traditional conception of learning. This trend is likely to continue as educators in primary and secondary schools gradually introduce more active forms of learning, use materials presented in a more imaginative way, draw on the available information and communication technologies (ICTs), and in general teach in a way that relates to the needs of learners, including, for example, their individual learning styles. In addition there is likely to be a shift away from assessment-driven learning in schools to a more flexible approach where independent learning is encouraged (QCA, 2007).

The teacher and teaching interventions

The teacher in FE and HE has experienced:

- a dramatic increase in the number of demanding students who come from diverse backgrounds and have high expectations of learning

- an increase in the number of students who need to be assessed

- a reduction in the number of staff compared with student figures

- an increase in external and internal assessments of teaching quality.

In addition, as younger students move into FE or HE they bring with them different norms, values and skills, in particular ICT skills and a familiarity with new media. Furthermore the regrading of polytechnics as universities has meant that people with a greater focus on teaching have joined the HE sector. These factors have encouraged a re-evaluation of current practice and a more professional approach to teaching and learning.

This has been reflected in the creation of more personalised, active learning environments that relate more to the needs of learners. This has been accompanied by a conscious effort to encourage independent learning and to develop the key transferable skills and aptitudes discussed above, partly through more attention being paid to vocational skills. In addition, greater use has been made of ICT, in particular virtual learning environments (VLEs). In turn these environments have enabled the incorporation of multimedia, discussion forums and so on. The development of teaching and learning material for these environments has also led to a reappraisal of how teaching materials should be delivered, incorporating ideas and good practice from domains such as human computer interface design, instructional design, e-learning and distance learning.

Among teachers there is also a genuine desire to create that 'magic moment' where learners engage with learning and gain new knowledge. This is accompanied by excitement and an appreciation of relevance, which are reflected in animated discussion and active participation. This is in itself a challenging desire bearing in mind the large number of students and relatively small number of teachers – compared with the past when there were fewer students and their backgrounds were more attuned to traditional academic study. Furthermore, even in research-led HE establishments it is increasingly unrealistic for academics to focus primarily on research and to treat teaching as an unfortunate necessity, partly because of the continuous institutional and public assessment of teaching quality. In Chapter 4 Jenny Yorke and Helen Walmsley suggest a possible way forward as they show how an online community of practice for teaching staff can be created and sustained.

A combination of these factors has led to a greater degree of rigour and an 'unpicking' of the practice of teaching and learning in FE and HE. Hence we are now seeing some systematic research into various aspects of teaching and learning, including the use of specific pedagogic practice – such as scaffolding, reflective practice, and the value of discourse, publication and peer-to-peer instruction – hoping to engage learners and encourage deep learning. In addition there is an exploration of new learning environments and strategies that foster learning, including problem-based learning, learning zones and e-discussion forums, and the role of teachers is changing to one of facilitator. The facilitator role in itself is challenging because it is unfamiliar, so teachers may experience feelings of loss of control and status. In Chapter 3 Geoff Walton suggests what the structure of a new e-pedagogy might look like in order to realise this challenge.

Tools and technologies

A host of new technologies is having an impact on the changing teaching and learning environment. These have evolved in recent years formally, for example as VLEs, and informally, for example as Web 2.0 technologies and freely accessible learning tools. The VLEs include software such as Blackboard and Moodle. The Web 2.0 technologies include software such as Facebook, Flickr, Twitter, YouTube, blogs and wikis. The freely accessible learning tools include applications such as note-taking software (e.g. NoteMesh), mind-mapping software (e.g. Thinkature), study guides (e.g. SparkNotes or Wikipedia) and bookmarking software (e.g. delicious). In addition there are freely available information retrieval tools such as Google, iBoogie, Exalead and Quintura, to name a few.

Many of these applications pose a challenge to formal learning environments. They tend to be easy to use and have evolved in a more user-centred way, often having a look, feel and functionality that directly address learners' needs. For example, they have an element of fun and informality, appealing to the emotional needs of learners. They have the ability to incorporate easily multimedia such as videos, which in themselves can draw on the power of narrative and face-to-face communication. In addition, some meet the cognitive needs of learners. For example, Quintura and WebBrain help users identify appropriate search terms, a cognitively complex task largely unsupported by traditional search tools such as academic online databases. Moodle provides a fresher interface that students are more likely to relate to, and has the ability to integrate a wide range of media including podcasts relatively easily, hence providing a learning environment that may relate to different learning styles and generally be more engaging.

Podcasts can be used to broadcast not only lectures but also, for example, videos of students reflecting on their learning, leading to peer-to-peer learning, which tends to engage students more than formal instruction by a person in authority. Facebook, an incredibly successful application (over 60 per cent of students at Loughborough University have a Facebook page), provides an excellent space for collaborative group work between students. Twitter, blogs and wikis provide a venue for self-publishing leading to individuals having a sense of being producers of knowledge and information as well as consumers. This can help learners feel that their work is valued and prepares them to be active contributors to a community of practice. Self-publication can also be used to encourage group- and self-reflection. However, not all students are comfortable with self-publication. They may feel self-conscious about stating their opinions or nervous of criticising others.

These technologies pose challenges and raise issues about privacy, quality control and how to integrate them into the formal learning environment. They also set a benchmark that students may use to judge the traditional learning environment. The setting up, monitoring and management of these tools can be extremely time-consuming, and the constant evolution of these applications is in itself demanding. For example, Second Life and other virtual reality multiplayer 'games' are currently being explored by teachers as possible learning environments. Brian Kelly in Chapter 5 and David Ley in Chapter 6 attempt to address some of these issues. David Ley in particular explores in some detail the new and emerging technologies at our collective disposal.

Conclusion

It can be seen that a host of factors – cultural and social, learners and their experience, teachers' professional knowledge, teachers' workplaces and evolving technologies – are having an impact on the teaching and learning environment. It is open to debate whether these factors are causal, coincidental or part of the interplay between the world around us and the sense we make of it or a combination of these factors.

In relation to the questions posed at the outset:

- Do the changes that have taken place reflect a reprioritisation of norms and values or are they something fundamentally new?
- Are the new technologies driving change or enabling us to do what we already know should be done?

it appears that primarily there has been a reprioritisation of norms and values. It is now possible to take advantage of the functionality offered by new technologies, and teaching and learners' experience will change for the better, so the needs of learners and society at large are met.

References

Hepworth, M. (2007) Knowledge of information behaviour and its relevance to the design of people-centred information products and services, *Journal of Documentation*, 63 (1), 33–56.

Hepworth, M. and Walton, G. (2009) *Teaching Information Literacy for Inquiry-based Learning*. Oxford: Chandos.

Howe, N. and Strauss, W. (2000) *Millennials Rising: the next generation*. New York: Vintage Books.

Prensky, M. (2001) Digital natives, digital immigrants, *On the Horizon*, 9 (5), *http://www.marcprensky.com/writing/Prensky% 20-%20Digital%20Natives,%20Digital%20Immigrants%20-% 20Part1.pdf* (accessed 8 November 2007).

QCA (2007) *14–19 Learning*, Qualifications and Curriculum Authority, *http://www.qca.org.uk/14-19/6th-form-schools/68_ 2462.htm* (accessed 8 November 2007).

Windham, C. (2005) The student's perspective. In D. G. Oblinger and J. L. Oblinger (eds), *Educating the Net Generation*. Washington, DC: Educause.

World Bank (2007) *Glossary, http://www.worldbank.org/depweb/ beyond/global/glossary.html#41* (accessed 8 November 2007).

2

Transforming the library – e-books and e-buildings
Dave Parkes

Introduction

Web 2.0 is transforming the library – its spaces, DNA, books and journals. It is changing how these resources are accessed, discovered and used. It is changing the fabric of libraries and their physical shape; the designed social spaces now common in libraries reflect online social networking spaces. Training, teaching and instruction in the use of libraries and learning resources are being transformed. Conversations, discourse, feedback and interaction with users through a variety of Web 2.0 tools are common and, importantly, two-way.

The book will eat itself – e-books 2.0

As I write physicists are about to engineer a collision of two beams of particles at something close to the speed of light in a big tunnel under the Swiss border with France. Assuming you are reading this and the Large Hadron Collider didn't open a black hole, which consumed us all, I will continue (update – I now know it didn't go quite according to plan and is either coming back from the future to destroy itself or bird detritus is getting in the way). What these physicists are also doing on this auspicious day is switching on 'the Grid'. The Grid is a worldwide grid of computers, combining the capacity of about 70,000 of the fastest computers in the world to analyse the millions of petabytes of data that will be generated. This data is equivalent to a 21-kilometre-high stack of CDs every year, according to the website (*http://lcg. web.cern.ch/LCG/lhcgridfest/*).

The last attempt to find the Higgs boson at CERN, 20 years ago, created a spin-off called the World Wide Web. This in turn set in motion the big, slow, radical transformation of libraries and its composite particle – the book. Who knows what the Grid may bring?

The e-book is now entering its late 30s and is undergoing a mid-life transformation. Born around 1971 in modest surroundings but with a good pedigree and a small but caring family in Project Gutenberg, its early years were quiet and understated, its teens geeky and awkward. The e-book now enters a kind of celebrity phase; it is becoming a household name and – like many celebrities – it remains elusive and yet ubiquitous, and is derided and applauded in equal measure.

What e-books could be – the online or networked book

The Institute for the Future of the Book (IFB; *http://www.futureofthebook.org/*) is describing a fascinating and compelling life for the online or networked book. This small 'think and do-tank' (their words) provides access to highly imaginative visual renderings of 'the book' in a fully realised hypertextual and interactive environment. These true e-books are captivating – they are different, but also strangely evocative of 'the book' – the codex – that 'perfect machine'.

In the hands of the IFB – just like a real book – the e-book becomes a powerful object, encouraging an intimate relationship with the reader, engaging the imagination and encouraging interaction. These IFB e-books allow access to the hinterland of the book, its contents, index, structure, narrative, size and mass. They allow readers to annotate, comment and interact with the book and the author. E-books are actually a joy to read and use online and highly recommended as a vision of what the 'networked book' can be.

McKenzie Wark published his book *Gamer Theory* (Wark, 2007) in two formats on the IFB website. One presents a text visualisation of the book called 'TextArc', a representation of the text: 'the entire text (twice!) on a single page'. It is a combination of an index, with every contextual occurrence of every word, and a summary. It uses the viewer's eye to help uncover meaning. In the other version, dubbed 'READ/WRITE', the pages are rendered as highly interactive cards, actually reminiscent of catalogue cards; it is very usable and lots of fun.

The book is also available in traditional hard copy format from Harvard University Press. These e-book models:

> pose the question of what digital technology can bring to the presentation of text. Are there new ways of perceiving text, or re-imagining text, that can only happen in the networked world? Could visualization change not only how we 'read' but how we write?
>
> Wark, 2007

Of course this isn't a model of a mass type or likely to become one just yet. Our e-books will continue to be, at least for the foreseeable future (six months – the definition of eternity in the web world?) rather flat digital replications of text. In our current dash for e-books are we simply buying (or leasing) a rendered digital facsimile of the book? It is really a photograph of an artefact – we are purchasing an image of the typing!

The e-book library – not reading but searching

Of course books don't stand alone – as librarians we are interested in building great libraries for our patrons – often against the odds. Alberto Manguel, in the foreword of his wonderful new book, *The Library at Night*, asks why we do this:

> Outside theology and fantastic literature, few can doubt that the main features of our universe are its dearth of meaning and lack of discernable purpose. And yet, with bewildering optimism, we continue to assemble whatever scraps of information we can gather in scrolls and books and computer chips, on shelf after library shelf, whether material, virtual or otherwise, pathetically intent on lending the world a semblance of sense and order.
>
> Manguel, 2008

He goes on to call libraries 'pleasantly mad places', which I think is a ringing endorsement of our craft.

E-books can provide an instant library – a library where we can weave and search through the texts of thousands of books from dozens of disciplines and in seconds. We can locate phrases, words, concepts and ideas. Books can now 'know' what other books contain. With algorithms we can penetrate connections and associations; waves and ripples are made – but this isn't reading – it's searching. I can search with speed and precision, in quantity and on demand, and the results are impressive. In 3.34 seconds I searched 20,000 e-books for 'Manguel' in a well-known aggregated e-book library, and returned 65 results across disciplines as diverse as folklore, political science, mathematics, heresy, education and the HBO series *The Sopranos*. This is incredibly powerful – but then, reader, the drudgery begins. I enter each book individually after launching the plug in (which only works on certain platforms and in certain browsers). The first is pleasant enough, I find the context and any other occurrences of Alberto Manguel, I can highlight and bookmark, add notes, but then I have to close this book and open another book and go through the process again; without some effort and patience I cannot cross-reference or compare texts or extracts. The search has promised so much but the rendition is a bore.

Borges wrote of the fantastical infinite library, containing the sum of all texts ever written. In *The Library of Babel* (2000) he writes of 'a someone' who was born in, spent his life in and knows he will die in the library – I can empathise with this poor citizen as I trawl around an e-library. Still, all the content we could want or ever need will eventually be available in there – and we must be imaginative about how we leverage and squirt this hidden content into the places and online spaces where people learn.

Every searcher a book, every book its e-book reader platform

Lots of different proprietary software and plugins are available to view e-books – some are streamed, never leaving the servers in Texas; others are downloaded. Platforms are often designed to build in digital rights management (DRM), the controversial access control mechanism, or they allow for extras like adding notes, or for citations and copyright statements to be printed.

Rapid developments in the functionality of web browsers such as in Firefox, Opera or Google Chrome leave the glacial and over-engineered development of some publisher platforms adrift in the primordial soup. Some aggregated e-libraries are still only fully functional with Microsoft's Internet Explorer for example.

There is a bewildering array of platforms and interfaces – just like with our e-journals collections in fact. Perhaps we need to recognise that journals and books are not so different in the 'e' world. E-content is more important than form; some integration would seem to be a sensible approach. For example, it would be a wonderful enhancement to be able to leap from a journal citation to an e-book chapter and back again with the minimum of fuss, but we seem to be some way from this.

Aggregators, suppliers and publishers have been slow to respond to or embrace new developments in emerging technologies or Web 2.0 applications, RSS aside. Librarians should adopt emerging standards or better still create or facilitate a 'mashup' of access to online content, which could really help transform the experience of reading online.

Devices and gadgetry

The IFB is weaving magic with online content but what about devices? There is now a proliferation of e-book readers available and more promised in the near future, all of which are intriguing and desirable objects. The successes of the Amazon Kindle in the USA and the Sony eBook Reader here in the UK are testament that there is a market for single niche devices. A number of so called 'Kindle

Killers' are now almost ready for release: companies such as Plastic Logic, Readius, Brother, Fujitsu and Barnes and Noble are all offering pocket-sized or A4 e-ink devices, some purported to be in colour and with wi-fi or 3G connectivity.

But how can we improve on that perfect machine – the book? Books are evocative, tactile, hypersensuous objects; we have a physical and a psychological relationship with them – they don't need wires, batteries, recharging or operating instructions – can a bleeping electronic device really replace or challenge the book? After all the book is highly portable, apart from some big computer manuals perhaps, and the world's largest book – currently *Bhutan: a visual odyssey* (this colossus weighs over 60 kg and measures 1.52 m by 2.13 m, oh, and the world's heaviest book, the 14,300 stone tablets recently rediscovered in China, published in AD 605).

How can these e-book readers improve on the reading experience? They can provide hundreds of titles in one portable, lightweight device. They allow the reader to change font size and page rendering and e-ink is easy on the eye. Devices will eventually allow for always-on access to the internet, for purchase or updating content. All very useful gadgetry but nothing a lightweight compact netbook couldn't offer?

It is assumed that sales of digital content will eventually outstrip sales of traditional books. A survey from the Frankfurt Bookfair in 2008 thinks this will happen by 2018 (Jones, 2008). Perhaps people will be encouraged to adopt e-readers more widely by the availability of e-news devices rather than e-books. In France (always early adopters – as evidenced by the prescient Minitel system – the pre-web online service) Orange has rolled out a paperless newspaper called Read & Go. This touchscreen device, about the size of a paperback, offers updates from five major newspapers including *Le Monde* and

Le Parisien. As a fundamental shift is taking place in the newspaper industry we could see revolutionary developments here. One possibility, recorded in the *Business Insider*, might be to give away the Kindle or a similar device and sell the newspaper as a wireless edition. According to the *Business Insider*, it costs the *New York Times* about twice as much money to print and deliver the newspaper over a year as it would cost to send each of its subscribers a brand new Amazon Kindle instead (Carlson, 2009).

Are single niche devices the way e-books will be delivered for our users or will we use multifunctional devices such as mobile phones or games consoles as our portable bookshelves of the near future?

I am reminded of the possibly apocryphal but nevertheless popular NASA pen story. This 'space pen' ballpoint was developed to be able to function in space at zero gravity. Taking years of development and costing millions of dollars to produce, it worked, but the Russians used a pencil.

Apple of course has the iPhone and the iPod Touch – this device is already proving to be the most popular e-book reader available. With the free download of Stanza (it also comes with one preloaded book, *The Time Machine* by H. G. Wells – very apt for this most futuristic of devices) you can read, resize, rotate and turn a page by flicking your finger, and download books over the web. A new free Kindle application is now available for the iPhone and iPod Touch to provide all the Kindle books available on the device.

There is a plethora of schemes and plans involving mobile phones. Borders has teamed up with Penguin and Bloomsbury to deliver the first chapters of novels to mobile phones for free. The DailyLit website (*http://www.dailylit.com/*) will send entire books in short customised instalments by e-mail or RSS to your phone, blackberry, iPhone or PC. The subscriber chooses the frequency and delivery mode. In Japan the 'keitai' – a novel for the mobile phone – is a phenomenon. Vodafone has launched a service bringing books to mobile phones in audio and text, and Google Book Search (*http://books.google.com/m*) now provides mobile editions.

E-publish or perish

The whole ecosystem is evolving and changing rapidly; publishers are seeking new revenue streams, suing (if press reports are to be believed) and courting upstart interlopers such as Scribd (*http://www.scribd.com*). Scribd is a document-sharing website with a social networking element; it has 55 million readers per month, and adds 50,000 documents per day. Simon and Schuster and Random House have teamed up to provide excerpts and full texts.

Publishers are experimenting with business models. Taylor & Francis allows users to 'rent' access to an e-book for a period of between a day and six months. Oxford Scholarship Online gives institutions subscription access to a fully searchable collection of 2,000 OUP monographs. And in 2009 Bloomsbury launched a set of e-books available as free downloads.

An interesting development is emerging in the shape of Flat World Knowledge. In this innovative model the publishing house gives textbooks away free online but sells study guides, paper versions, flash cards and versions for the Kindle. The textbooks are built to order, allowing the mixing of content. An online social learning platform is also included as is a Blackboard and Facebook application (*http://www.flatworldknowledge.com/minisite/*).

OverDrive is a global digital distributor which libraries can sign up to, as 8,500 have done. This service provides 150,000 downloadable audiobook, e-book, video and music titles. In 2008 it registered approximately 5.3 million checkouts of digital material, a 76 per cent increase over 2007 (*http://www.overdrive.com/*).

Google Books – the infinite library

The big e-book news has to be the Google agreement with the book industry. Google now has 20,000 publishers participating in its book-scan programme. This means that users will soon be able to search and buy millions of titles, many of which were out of print and previously unobtainable. The scheme will be targeted at universities but will allow anyone to download any of the 7 million books already scanned by Google.

Google won't be an infinite library just yet, however. Google's CEO Eric Schmidt estimates that it won't manage to index all of the world's information until around the 24th century (Mills, 2005).

The future observed

As the Joint Information Systems Committee (JISC) national e-books observatory project discovered, there is clearly a demand for e-course texts, which is currently not being met (JISC, 2008). Concerns over the impact of e-course books on print sales and uncertainty about a sustainable pricing model are still holding things back. According to Mintel (2007), academic and professional books were an estimated 20 per cent of the total market in 2007. As this is in a market worth £3,414 million, one can understand the risk aversion.

We are entering a transformative era, though, and witness to a key moment in the evolution of publishing and digital libraries as each word in each book is cross-linked, clustered, cited, extracted, indexed, analysed, annotated, remixed and reassembled; every bit informs another; every page reads all the other pages. Edward A. Feigenbaum, a noted Artifical Intelligence pioneer, wrote in 1989 from the perspective of a future scholar who recollects the time 'when books didn't talk to each other': 'The library of the future will be a network of knowledge systems in which people and machines collaborate' (Feigenbaum and Merritt, 1989).

What is clear is that the e-book in all of its manifestations is undergoing what mathematicians, biologists and economists call a 'random walk' (one version is the drunkard's walk – but we won't explore that further). We know successive random steps are being made and we can try to model the outcomes and build innovative and adaptive services, but the real outcome remains unknown – perhaps the answer lies in what is happening at CERN and in 'the Grid'.

If there were no such thing as libraries would we build them today?

Just as the DNA of the library – the book – is morphing, so too are our buildings being terraformed and transformed into creative, dynamic, technologically rich, inspirational, motivational and aspirational places, which encourage social interaction, inquiry-based learning, collaborative activity, coffee, cakes and cultural opportunities.

This physical reinvention complements and reflects the virtual emergent social media phenomenon we have experienced online over the last five years of Web 2.0. Social media, blogging, microblogging, social networking, social bookmarking, tagging and the wisdom of crowds all combine elements that are supported by physical manifestations in the shape of new library buildings. For example, librarians recognise that libraries are not built purely for administrative simplicity but they need to foster human to human interaction, communication, knowledge syndication, inquiry, collaboration, discussion and consultation in places where people not only consume but produce content, media and knowledge. The new library is a social interface as much as Facebook or Google Wave.

As Facebook and other social networking tools are virtual community spaces, these new learning spaces are physical community spaces. Barry Wellman (1979) described communities as 'as networks of interpersonal ties that provide sociability, support, information, a sense of belonging, and social identity'. This definition can be applied to online communities as well as the activities and services encouraged in new libraries.

Architecture and libraries share a special relationship; the great libraries of the world have the ability to inspire, uplift, engage, stimulate thought and evoke emotions. They are cultural and political symbols, and libraries remain great assets for universities as a special place, a third place.

Libraries which were once designed for administrative simplicity are now designed for user experience. These new libraries are a big experiment, just as our forays into emerging and social technologies are experimental discoveries. They are beta buildings, where ideas are implemented and iterated – always morphing and evolving to reflect and engender change.

Should library administration even manage these new spaces? Why not the students' union, or student services, estates, IT or even Starbucks? What do librarians bring which cannot just as easily be delivered by another agency? Certainly we identify, select and manage information and learning resources and pay the bills, but increasingly the information we buy goes straight from the supplier to the end user without needing to 'enter' the building.

The connected building

We shape our buildings; thereafter they shape us.

Winston Churchill

New library design is increasingly important in supporting innovations in learning, pedagogy and improving learners' experience.

There has been considerable national investment in 'library' spaces in the last few years. 'Designing Libraries', the Aberystwyth University based database for sharing best practice in the planning and design of library spaces, lists 473 projects including 187 new builds and 202 refurbishments since 2004 (*http://www.designinglibraries.org.uk/*). New library design is increasingly important in supporting innovations in learning, pedagogy and improving learners' experience. The new library is at the intersection of the physical and the virtual; it is a democratic building. In this new democratic building there is an ingrained culture of openness.

Let us take a 'walk' through this connected building of dynamic interaction, scholarly activity, mobile communications, pervasive computing and ubiquitous wireless. On entry, video walls display scrolling directions and news, another video wall displays real time tweets from users of the library explaining what they are up to or looking for in the building or across the university; this facilitates interaction and sparks new conversation. Augmented reality tags installed at critical points in the journey provide smart phone users with tours of the building and inform users how the space and services might be used, where certain resources or help might be found. Throughout library users provide crowdsourced and backchannel feeds on screens describing good finds, tips, help and advice on using the library; and online photographs are geotagged to show the locations of resources or services. QR codes lead smart phone users to content, books and resources. The building is fractal, agile, changing to suit the demands of learners and the academic calendar. For example, high use services around assignment deadlines such as short loan, binding and printing can be co-located for convenience, and moved back to more traditional and familiar locations once the frenzy has subsided. Experiments with bokodes (*http://www.bokode.com*) provide users with information about the book stock and journals collections, information previously only accessible by administrative and library staff.

Large interactive touch screens allow instant access to resources. Capture cams record group work scribblings. Geotagged photographs of the building are just some of the ways that user generated information pervades – the richness of any building is most apparent to those who use it. Wireless power mats using magnetic induction charge devices for users. Expresso book machines print and bind books on demand. Devices have communication and computing capabilities, connected to other information devices in the environment and to other people. There is embedded technology in everything from books to furniture to the building itself. In the main gathering area there is a recital, and yet there is a refuge of silence and scholarship away from the cacophony and electric hum in the silent study area.

This is a place where the web meets the world (O'Reilly and Battelle, 2009), where occupiers feel part of a collective whole; they can influence and effect change and contribute to the stimulus of their surroundings. It is a highly symbolic place for the university in increasing motivation, productivity, recruitment and retention. It demonstrates at least some elements of sustainability and an awareness of carbon emissions.

Libraries were always more than book repositories. They have always been social learning spaces for people to study, gather, work collaboratively and interact with resources and technology. They have always addressed space and design issues through technology and improved design, whether by providing microform and film to liberate space 60 years ago or through the use of papyrus scrolls some time before that. Libraries were always a forum for meetings, sharing information, educating, agitating, organising and entertaining. In the early nineteenth century they were sometimes called mechanics institutes or perhaps the Athenaeum; now we call them learning resource centres, information commons, knowledge centres, knowledge hubs or idea stores.

Libraries have always been a forum rather than a scriptorium. Recitals, exhibitions, meetings and workshops have been the stuff of libraries in all sectors through the ages – the journey of the library is now reaching its apogee in the shape of the 'Get it Loud in Libraries' campaign by Lancaster public library, which since 2005 has staged live band concerts in among the book shelves. By sparking controversy it has also generated great interest and encouraged 3,500 young people into the library who otherwise might never have visited. Lancaster is not alone: this is happening in libraries from Auckland to Wigan and Wokingham.

This decision by bands to play more gigs in ever more diverse places and for libraries to open their doors to welcome them is a direct and unimagined consequence of web technologies creating paradigm shifts in the respective industries. In the music industry the web has changed the business model and in libraries the very idea of a library is being questioned to the extent that we can in all seriousness ask: 'If libraries didn't exist would we build them today?'

References

Borges, J. L. (2000) *The Library of Babel*. Boston, MA: David R. Godine; Enfield: Airlift, 2000.

Bradwell, P. (2009) *The Edgeless University*. London: Demos.

Carlson, N. (2009) Printing the NYT costs twice as much as sending every subscriber a free Kindle, *Business Insider*, 30 January, *http://www.businessinsider.com/2009/1/printing-the-nyt-costs-twice-as-much-as-sending-every-subscriber-a-free-kindle* (accessed 26 March 2009).

CIBER (2007) *Information Behaviour of the Researcher of the Future*, *http://www.ucl.ac.uk/infostudies/research/ciber/downloads/GG%20BL%20Learning%20Report.pdf* (accessed 21 December 2009).

Committee of Inquiry into the Changing Learner Experience (2009) *Higher Education in a Web 2.0 World: report of an independent committee of inquiry into the impact on higher education of students' widespread use of Web 2.0 technologies*, *http://www.jisc.ac.uk/media/documents/publications/heweb20r ptv1.pdf* (accessed 21 December 2009).

Feigenbaum, J. and Merritt, M. (1989) *Distributed Computing and Cryptography: proceedings of a DIMACS workshop*, DIMACS Series in Discrete Mathematics and Theoretical Computer Science 2. Providence, RI: American Mathematical Society.

JISC (2008) *JISC National E-books Observatory Project*, Joint Information Systems Committee, *http://www.jiscebooksproject .org/* (accessed 10 October 2008).

Jones, P. (2008) Industry divided over digitisation, *Bookseller*, 10 October, *http://www.thebookseller.com/news/68796-industry-divided-over-digitisation-.html* (accessed 17 October 2008).

Latimer, K. and Niegaard, H. (2007) *IFLA Library Building Guidelines: developments & reflections*. Munich: K. G. Saur.

Manguel, A. (2008) *The Library at Night*. London: Yale University Press.

Mills, E. (2005) Google ETA? 300 years to index the world's info, CNET News, 8 October, *http://news.cnet.com/Google-ETA-300-years-to-index-the-worlds-info/2100-1024_3-5891779.html* (accessed 10 October 2008).

Mintel (2007) *Books*. London: Mintel Group.

O'Reilly, T. and Battelle, T. (2009) *Web Squared: Web 2.0 five years on, http://assets.en.oreilly.com/1/event/28/web2009_ websquared-whitepaper.pdf* (accessed 21 December 2009).

University of Rochester (2007) *Studying Students: the undergraduate research project at the University of Rochester, http://hdl.handle.net/1802/7520* (accessed 21 December 2009).

Wark, M. (2007) *Gamer Theory*. Cambridge, MA: Harvard University Press.

Wellman, B. (1979) The community question, *American Journal of Sociology*, 84, 1201–31.

Part 2:
People

3

Online social networking, the e-learning holy grail?

Geoff Walton

Introduction

The study reported in this chapter shows that students regard online collaborative learning (online social network learning; OSNL) motivating, productive and enjoyable, which tutors have found leads students to a better understanding of their subject. This chapter seeks to argue that the lessons learnt from this research can be harnessed to provide us with a generic template for managing online discourse, a protocol for using any online social networking Web 2.0 application for educational purposes. This generic template is, in effect, a new e-pedagogy for participative learning, which is platform independent and employs the positive social connectivity features that Web 2.0 provides.

Recent research supports the view that the e-learning 'holy grail' in higher education is to engage students in online discourse, whether student-to-student dialogue or student-to-tutor dialogue, or both, arguing that active involvement promotes effective learning (Webb et al., 2004). Work in this sector in the UK using discussion boards in the Blackboard virtual learning environment (VLE), notably Walton et al. (2007a and b), Pope and Walton (2009) and Hepworth and

Walton (2009), corroborate this view. The empirical evidence furnished here supports the views stated in chapters 5 and 6 on the potential of Web 2.0 to deliver meaningful learning. It also complements the work of Jenny Yorke and Helen Walmsley (Chapter 4) on the use of communities of practice to foster staff development in e-learning and e-pedagogy. Indeed, the work discussed here features in discussions about the online community of practice explored in Chapter 4.

Background to the study

Information Services at Staffordshire University (UK) has delivered information literacy in traditional face-to-face format within the year one undergraduate sport and exercise module SHP91000-1 Effective Learning, Information and Communication Skills (ELICS) for five years. It should be noted that although the topic of information literacy is in itself interesting, a discussion of the concept itself is beyond the scope of this chapter. A working definition of information literacy is offered for the purposes of this study. It is argued that, in essence, information literacy is the ability to find, evaluate and use information in order to complete a task. This chapter centres on how students used online social network learning to understand how to critically evaluate information sources more effectively. Recent work by UCL (2008), CELEX (2009), Hampton-Reeves et al. (2009) and Head and Eisenberg (2009) continues to demonstrate the need for this kind of information literacy teaching and learning in education: 'digital natives' are not the same as information literate learners (Williams and Rowlands, 2006).

In the past, information literacy skills were delivered face to face and tended to focus on these skills in a generic fashion rather than via a learner-orientated mode where thinking skills and subject-specific information literacy were promoted.

Information literacy activity-based exercises were assessed through an individual portfolio exercise with no built-in opportunity for collaboration or discussion. Understandably (because of the generic nature of the skills learned and the lack of opportunity for structured discussion), incidental student feedback indicates that students had difficulty in perceiving the benefit of these generic exercises and therefore felt less motivated to take part in them.

These issues led the researcher and module leader to believe that it was time for a change. It was envisaged that students would develop a more positive attitude towards their learning if tutors delivered information literacy activities using collaborative learning opportunities, particularly when the activities were subject based and linked seamlessly to the goal of undertaking professional research in sport and exercise.

In the face-to-face workshop this was realised by using a scaffolded framework (following resources developed for this purpose by Bordinaro and Richardson, 2004) where students (individually and collaboratively) were encouraged to identify their research focus, find, evaluate and use information within a specific subject-related context and reflect on the process (following structures suggested by Cowan, 2002), thereby creating a more subject orientated motivational atmosphere.

It was of particular interest whether this positive motivational context, as suggested by Keller (1983), could be further enhanced (and learning improved) by using online social network learning via the Blackboard VLE. Goodyear (2001), JISC infoNet (2004), Littlejohn and Higgison (2003) and Mayes and de Freitas (2004) indicate that, in the online context, learning only takes place when students are encouraged to engage in dialogue with peers and tutors and these authors regard this as e-learning best practice. E-group etiquette guidelines set out by Alpay (2005) in tandem with notions about reflective practice (following Teles, 1993;

Hung and Chen, 2001; Cowan, 2002; and Walker, 2003) and communities of practice espoused by Mayes and de Freitas (2004) were followed to enable the online discourse between students and their peers and student and tutor to be meaningful and sustained.

It was argued that by using Blackboard discussion board in this way the 'tertiary courseware' function (Goodyear, 2001) where learners produce materials during their discussions and assessment of their own learning would be created. For example, online dialogue between learner and tutor or peer discussion outputs would be captured and made available to all learners.

Pilot study

A full account of the pilot study can be found in Walton et al. (2007a and b).

Methodology

To test whether online social network learning really did make a difference to student learning the activities were delivered to an experimental group via Blackboard over seven weeks immediately after the face-to-face workshop. In addition, a control group, which received the face-to-face workshop only, was monitored to enable a comparison between online social network learning and traditional delivery methods. In effect the experimental group received a 'blended learning' programme – a mixture of face-to-face and online activities. The structure for the whole blended programme (in chronological order) and the data-gathering instruments are represented in Figure 3.1. In addition to these the textual output from the discussion board in the form of student postings and summaries was captured at the time by copying and pasting all discourse into a Word document.

The initial process devised to manage the online social network learning information literacy activities in discussion board within Blackboard is represented in Figure 3.2.

Brief summary of findings from the pilot study

The outputs from the online social network learning information literacy activities were very encouraging and a new process for managing these emerged. Students produced some excellent output that could be used as threads for many of the subsequent online social network learning activities, for example, a scaffolded discussion was developed by selecting a student comment regarding URLs (from OSNL 4). This was then used as the thread for OSNL 5 by reiterating the previous discussion, but this time in more detail. This is an extract from the student posting used:

> You can check the URL of a web page to see if it's an educational piece or a personal piece which contains someone's own opinion.

The subsequent task derived from the student comment was posted as follows:

> It was mentioned in the previous discussion that you can check the URL of a web page to work out its origin, for example, educational, personal, commercial, governmental, sporting organisation etc. So what is a URL and how do you work out its origin?

Hence, students were reiterating the task completed during the previous week, but in much greater depth. This demonstrated that there was a recursive element to this activity, which was harnessed for future online discussions. This process of iteration is mentioned as an essential part of

Figure 3.1 Information literacy blended programme and data-gathering instruments

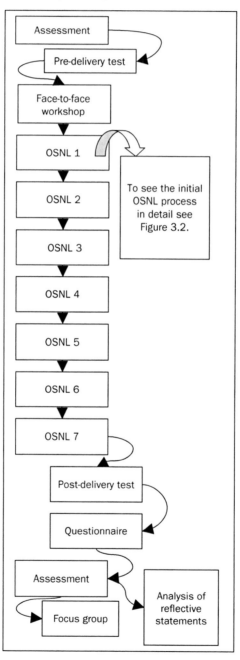

Figure 3.1	Information literacy blended programme and data-gathering instruments (Cont'd)

Assessment: A problem-based scenario, which directed students to identify and evaluate two websites, two books or e-books, and two journal or e-journal articles to deliver a talk to A-level students on football hooliganism. This contextualised the whole information literacy delivery.

Pre-delivery test: Administered at the start of the workshop; this comprised 11 questions which tested students' knowledge of the library catalogue, searching e-journals and evaluating information, following Andretta (2005).

Face-to-face workshop: 50-minute workshop including a demonstration on searching the library catalogue, a whole group discussion on identifying keywords (including identifying synonyms, e.g. soccer or football), a demonstration of SwetsWise using simple Boolean searching, a worksheet of tasks (mirroring the assessment) and a plenary where students discussed their answers.

OSNL 1 [online social network learning activity 1]: An online reflective practice task of answering three questions: 'What did I actually learn in this session today?', 'Which were the most difficult parts and why were they difficult for me?' and 'Which were the most straightforward parts and why did I find these easy?' The initial process for managing each of these activities (OSNL 1–7) is represented in Figure 3.2.

OSNL 2: This focused on devising general evaluation criteria for judging information sources.

OSNL 3: In order to scaffold and seed this activity a statement was produced from summarised responses from OSNL 2, which generated the questions used to focus students on more detailed issues of evaluation.

OSNLs 4 and 5: The scaffolded activity for OSNL 4 was drawn from a different student posting made in OSNL 2, enabling us to focus on OSNL 4 (on evaluating web page content) and OSNL 5 (a more detailed evaluation question about decoding URLs).

OSNL 6: This activity focused on referencing sources.

OSNL 7: An online reflective practice task, which asked students to look back over all the online social network learning activities, answer two questions on what skills they had developed and how they would apply them, post a response and then comment on a fellow student's posting.

Post-delivery test: Administered at the end of the workshop, comprising the pre-delivery test questions to detect differences in knowledge.

Questionnaire: Administered after the post-delivery test to gain students' views on the online social network learning activities.

Assessment: Students were required to provide six resources with a short evaluation of each and a 150-word reflective practice statement on the skills they had learned and how they would apply them.

Focus group: A one-hour interview held in Semester 2 with five students chosen at random from the experimental group. Questions were based on questionnaire responses.

Analysis of reflective statements: Reflective statements were analysed using content analysis methods based on Huberman and Miles (1994).

Figure 3.2 Initial process for managing online social network learning

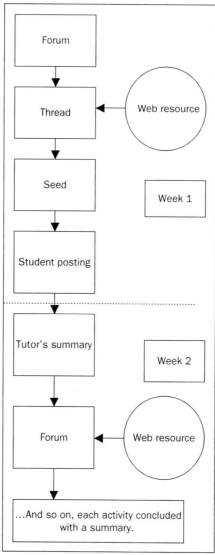

Forum: This constitutes the title, e.g. 'Referencing your sources'.
Thread: This contains the instructions for the task, e.g.: '1 Think about what you have covered today. 2 Answer the questions set out below. 3 Send your response to the discussion board. 4 Read the responses your fellow students have made and make at least one comment.'

| **Figure 3.2** | Initial process for managing online social network learning (*Cont'd*) |

Seed: This contains the starting point for the discussion, e.g.: 'It was mentioned in the previous discussion that you can check the URL of a web page to work out its origin – whether educational, personal, commercial, governmental, sporting organisation etc. What is a URL and how do you work out its origin?'
Student posting: This is the output from students once they have opened the forum, read the thread and seed, and engaged with the online activity, e.g.: 'I would judge a book by determining how referenced the book is and what references it included.'
Tutor's summary: This summary contains salient points raised from student postings with additional comments from tutors, e.g.: 'You have identified some excellent criteria – we have added some extra points you should consider when using web pages. General point: there are no guarantees that any web page is unbiased, error free or reputable but if you adhere to the criteria you have put forward – summarised below – then you should get a reasonable idea as to how reliable the source is.'
  This was envisaged as a linear process with each activity concluded and closed with a summary before moving on to the next new forum. The threads were generated each week by tutors, so the content was tutor led.

Source: Walton et al., 2007a, 17

information literacy in, for example, SCONUL (1999), Big Blue Project (2002) and Andretta (2005), as part of the information behaviour process in, for example Hepworth (2004) and Ford (2004), and as part of the learning process in, for example, Laurillard (2002) and Moseley et al. (2004). Finally, it has the desirable outcome of making the process student rather than tutor led, allowing the programme to adopt a more constructivist approach to learning.

It can be seen that the literature anticipated this occurrence of the iterative nature of the online discussion task (and learning itself) but was not planned for in the original process. As a result, a new process map was devised for managing online discussion for the main study, which is illustrated in Figure 3.3.

It can be assumed that there was no 'social desirability bias' (Bryman, 2004): students were not averse to making negative as well as positive comments or statements:

Some of the activities were a bit useless.

In fact the majority of questionnaire statements were positive. For example this typical statement strongly indicates that the referencing exercise was the most successful online social network learning activity:

> I think learning about references was useful and improved my understanding of it.

A typical response to the question about what they found not so useful was:

> I did not find reflecting on the work of another useful.

This showed that the online reflective practice activity required further work.

In the questionnaire 11 of the 16 respondents made one or more negative statements about the online reflective practice activity. This suggests that students may have tacit expectations that learning should be provided by 'experts' such as tutors and that they can't possibly learn anything from their peers.

Responses indicated that none of the students had looked at the tutor summaries after completion of the online activity, demonstrating that it was necessary to find an alternative process for presenting these.

Pre- and post-delivery tests produced no statistically significant differences in marks although, gratifyingly, post-delivery test scores were higher.

An analysis of the written reflective statements can be found in Walton et al. (2007b).

Changes to processes for the main study

Students in the pilot study commented that the online social network learning activities were 'repetitive' and 'tedious'. It was also observed that in OSNL 6 the numbers of secondary postings were far greater than any of the other online social network learning activities. OSNL 6 was the only discussion held over two weeks. Therefore, it was felt that fewer online social network learning activities should be deployed in the main study and each should take place over at least two weeks to minimise repetition and maximise the available time for students to engage in the discussion.

In addition, following recommendations made by the Plain English Campaign website a number of changes to online activity instructions were made. The main recommendations were: use short sentences, use simple words, refrain from using jargon and use an active 'voice' where possible. These recommendations were deployed for the seeds and threads of online social network learning activities in particular. Following recommendations by Nicol, Minty and Sinclair (2003), tutor summaries were made more personal using students' and tutors' first names (to identify the origin of online postings) and using coloured text or bold to separate students' comments from tutors' comments as illustrated here:

> Tracy said that a good resource should consist of many different points of view, which allows us to assess it against our own work.
>
> **We would add that bias is minimised by using evidence to back up the points that are made with detailed explanations of the information that is needed (in other words lots of facts and figures).**

Placing these summaries before a task or activity within the same online document will ensure that students read the summary before reading the instructions for the new task. In addition students will be given the summary as a printed handout for future reference.

It was decided to construct a reflective multiple-choice quiz in the form of an instant reflective practice activity (IRPA) rather than an open-ended reflection. These activities were designed to take up to ten minutes to complete and enabled students to reflect actively on their learning. They contained 'ready made' reflective statements for students to select, enabling them to see how to construct a reflective practice statement for their assessed work. The 'ready made' reflective statements were created using reflective statements made by previous students. It was felt that by using real reflective statements students would identify with and consequently choose at least one that was provided, or else write their own. The structure for the new information literacy programme is shown in Figure 3.3.

Figure 3.3 Scheme for the new information literacy programme indicating new features

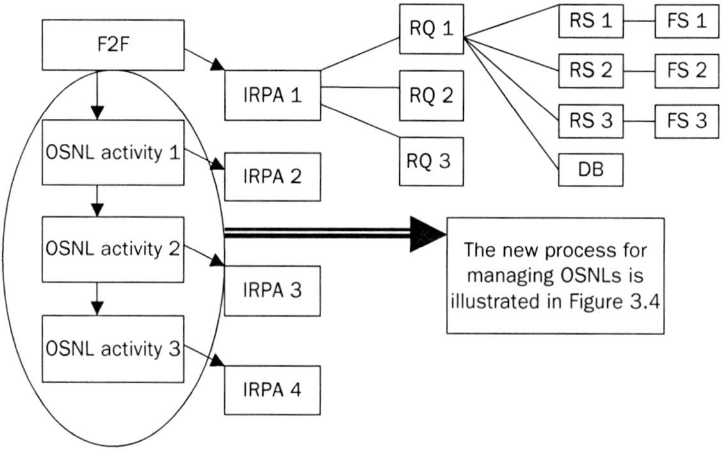

Key

F2F: Face-to-face workshop session
OSNL activity: Online social network learning activity
IRPA: Instant reflective practice activity
RQ: Reflective question
RS: Reflective statement (two statements only presented in IRPAs 2–4)
DB: Dialogue box for students to make a reflective statement in their own words
FS: Feedback statement

Source: adapted from Walton et al., 2007b, 197

44

To replicate the findings of the pilot study and take advantage of the new online social network learning process that emerged, it is recommended that the online social network learning process is managed as shown in Figure 3.4.

Figure 3.4 New process for managing student centred online social network learning activities

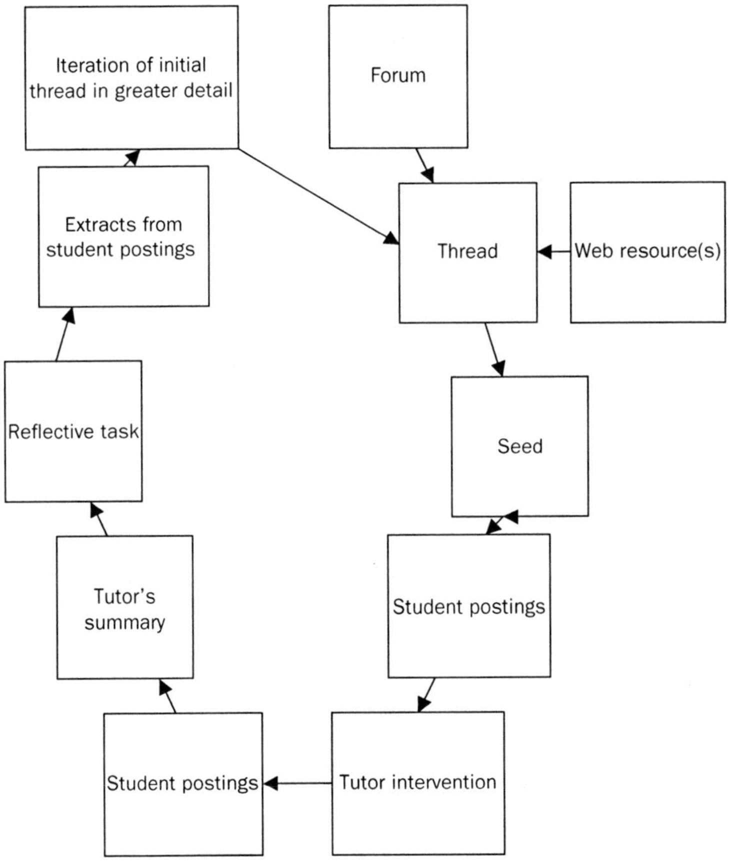

Iteration of initial thread in greater detail

Forum

Extracts from student postings

Thread

Web resource(s)

Reflective task

Seed

Tutor's summary

Student postings

Student postings

Tutor intervention

Source: Walton et al., 2007b, 200

Main study

Methodology

The online social network learning activities were delivered to the experimental group via Blackboard over six weeks immediately after the face-to-face workshop. In tandem the control group received only the face-to-face delivery. A third group received the face-to-face delivery and access to the interactive web resources but were not given access to the OSNL activities on the discussion board. The structure for the new programme is shown above in Figure 3.3. The new online social network learning process was managed as shown in Figure 3.4 and data-gathering instruments were reused including any changes described above.

Findings

Online discourse

Students readily engaged in the online activities provided and all those present made a contribution. They tended to use their own words and identified a range of appropriate evaluation criteria which they could use when gathering web pages for an assignment:

> I would evaluate a web page by: looking at the URL address and seeing weather [sic] it is e.g. a government source, which would mean the source is reliable. You can also look at the author and find out whether they have a good reliable background and you should also be able to find any related links and other sources used. Finally look at the last time when the web page was updated especially when stats are involved.

The average length of a posting was 66 words with at least two salient points per posting. Students tended to focus on relevance above any other criterion, but many mentioned authority, reliability, currency and the importance of being able to understand a URL, which was a remarkable achievement as the allotted time to undertake activities rarely exceeded 15 minutes.

The pilot study findings on moments of iteration were replicated and provided opportunities to explore issues in more depth. This extract from the tutor's summary demonstrates how this was achieved:

> Ozzy mentioned that you can get clues from a URL to see whether it is a 'personal' website and (therefore) the information may not be a reliable source.
>
> **We agree with Ozzy regarding URLs BUT stress that we need to be more systematic in the way we analyse their structure. To practise analysing a URL follow the instructions 1–5 below.**

This in turn led to students posting more detailed comments on how to analyse a URL:

> The URL informs us that it is an online article from an academic server (.ac) based in the United Kingdom (.uk). It tells us that the website contains football research and resources (/resources) with factsheets (/factsheets). The end of the URL shows us that the article is a html file (.html).

Tutors then summarised all pertinent comments into a brief handout to act as an *aide-mémoire* for evaluating web pages for their assignments.

Students' views on the information literacy online social network learning programme

The focus group interviews and questionnaire generated a large body of data. Only selected transcriptions are presented here, in an attempt to give as accurate a representation of students' views as possible.

Comments from student respondents confirmed that they felt that the online social network learning task was framed at the right level:

> Easy to follow because obviously I did the activity so it didn't go over my head, explained what I needed to do and went about doing it.

Students quickly took on the role of online learners and understood what was required:

> Made our replies on the forum, we had to feedback on each others. I remember I was commenting on his, he was commenting on mine and I was writing about how he hadn't actually written about all the actual points you were meant to evaluate.

What began to emerge was that students regarded the activity as a rewarding learning experience:

> Obviously you feel something productive like you've done some work and you've done something useful like you've learnt stuff and then you've like soaked up the information then you've managed to like extract it in the reply for other people to see in the forum.

Students seemed readily to transfer the norms associated with face-to-face discourse into the online environment:

> Everybody's got limits ain't they and you've got to respect the other person's opinion and they have to respect your opinion at the end of the day.

Within the online social network learning environment students showed that they quickly achieved a sense of what was required in this setting:

> I went into the link about what you should look for when you go onto the internet websites and using them as references, and taking that information and then so I took all that in then basically just wrote a few paragraphs on what I thought was important.

The activity appeared to get students to think about what was being written by their fellow students:

> The opinions got on it were really, really good. I read through everybody's really, and I seen what everyone was getting at and it made me understand more clearly because at first, as I said before, I didn't get it, it didn't click. That helped by reading other people's statements on the activity so it worked better for me.

In addition, an interesting debate arose in the full focus group meeting on what constituted the most important criteria for judging web pages. Students concurred that by doing the online social network learning task they had become sensitised to these issues.

These statements show how detailed students' knowledge had become when they analysed web pages:

> Looking at URL, e.g. .com/.uk, taught me that website URLs mean something important.

> I learnt how to assess a website by simply looking at the web address, date published, author etc.

> [Before] I didn't know what the things at the end like .ac [and] .org meant.

It should be noted that the experimental group performed statistically significantly better in the post-delivery test than the control group (p<0.025). It is our contention that this indicates that online social network learning does promote deeper learning in students for information-literacy-based activities.

As identified by Hepworth (2004), in cognitive terms evidence from respondents showed that in this learning context they had moved from a position of uncertainty to one of certainty:

> It was good because I didn't really know about what type of things you should look for when you are looking at websites to get references so now obviously when I'm looking at references in the future I'm going to look and see whether it is from a big company where it's very probably going to be factual or whether it's from someone's own personal website or something that's less formal and I'll be able to tell whether to take information from it or not.

Students' responses also demonstrated that they had begun to adopt a more questioning approach as a result of the activity:

> Allowed me to see what other people thought of the web site, the way they had evaluated it, not just myself. Then you got, obviously, to post a reply to them saying

well look at this, look at that, and also got their feedback to yours.

You got to see what you was missing out or something you hadn't looked at, so they could bring up the points saying may be look at this, look at this.

Almost all student interview comments and questionnaire responses were positive. It emerges very clearly that students thought the pedagogic intervention was useful and that it helped them to learn:

Yeah, it's a good idea I think, it gets people quite motivated to do things because they can see next week they get involved, it's more hands-on and they can actually see that what they did is actually being used for the good really.

However, a minority of students made negative comments:

Not much really. No I can't remember, I probably wasn't here.

Some activities were not interesting.

It also appears that students felt very positive towards the activity and felt that they had a real part to play in it:

It was really good, you got to see what other people thought of their web site and you could have a look at different web sites and different people's opinions, which was really good.

I think it was quite interesting, gets you involved as well and that side of it was quite fun – as opposed to being lectured to.

Students' views on the tutor's summary reinforced this view:

> Just a nice way of being recognised, basically it was really nice knowing it wasn't just being done for you to write up and to be left. It was nice knowing it was going to be read through, all the reflective stuff was, and actually being given a report on it.

It is argued that by creating a positive and motivational atmosphere in this way learning is more likely to occur.

Research from learning theory (Race, 2001) and thinking skills work (Moseley et al., 2004) shows that in order to facilitate learning metacognitive processes should be evident. Online social network learning discourse appears to initiate this process in that students feel they have missed or overlooked something and realise there is something else to know:

> You got to see what other people thought about... your evaluation, get new points in case you missed anything.

> Somebody commenting on your evaluation and you could possibly highlight things that you overlooked.

These statements appear to indicate that the online social network learning process has enabled students to identify gaps in their information seeking, or in information literacy terms to recognise a need to find more information, which provide the moments of iteration (Walton et al., 2007a) and the motivation to continue enabling further opportunities for discussion and hence learning.

The following statements indicate the realisation or recognition that new knowledge had been acquired:

> Quite informative, something I weren't [sic] aware of. I was aware that there was a lot of pages but I was

under the impression they were all .co.uk. You actually realise there are quite a lot of organisations that put web pages online. It's good I suppose when you are researching, you don't want to put lies in your assignment and stuff, you want to put truth in there.

It helped me recognise weaknesses in my study skills.

Referencing correctly – didn't realise how many ways there was.

The process was then closed off by completing the reflective activity:

I remember it [the IRPA], basically asking you how you felt or what you learnt doing the workshop. You can reflect yourself, then it's not just reflecting for a lecturer it's, like, you can understand yourself what you have learnt and gone through.

However, students weren't entirely at ease with the instant reflective practice activity and didn't entirely engage with or value it:

The workshop was useful to me, but I think, like, that one [the IRPA] was more of a getting my views on, on things and stuff, so not really that useful to me. It questioned my opinion on the workshop I suppose. I was just giving my opinion, it didn't really learn [sic] me anything.

Students' responses indicated that in completing this activity their behaviour had changed and learning had taken place:

It makes you aware, a little bit more aware, of what web sites are more useful to you than others and there are quite a lot of web sites on line and you don't want to be writing stuff in your assignments that's not true.

Many students commented that they would use their new knowledge in their future undergraduate career and had already used it in other modules:

> It was quite informative actually. I learnt quite a few things... I've used it for a couple of my essays and a lab report I'm doing at the moment.

Finally, students liked the fact that their efforts were recognised and included, not just in the tutor's summary but also in the handout given to them as an *aide-mémoire*. It appeared to create a real sense of ownership:

> I thought it was really good, obviously. It gave the whole group a bit of recognition, you could see individuals what they'd done what they'd said, but it also helped you read through what other people thought of URLs and took advice from other people not just the lecturer. It worked really well, it is a good way of reflecting what you've done.

Discussion

The findings indicated that student participants readily engaged with the tasks and seemed to enjoy them. The activities appeared to capture students' interest, which was evidenced in the level of participation and the quality of the output. They appeared to realise the relevance of the skills to them as they could see how the skills could be applied in other modules and in later years. In particular they appeared to show signs of becoming critical thinkers and what Senn

Breivik calls 'information sceptics' (Brower and Hollister, 2007), a key milestone on becoming information literate.

The fact that students in the experimental group had performed statistically significantly better in the knowledge test than the control group is further indication that this intervention has been beneficial. The tutor's summary appeared to create a sense of success and ownership by recognising students' efforts and reinforcing them in a positive way.

These findings suggest that the conditions required to meet Keller's ARCS (attention, relevance, confidence and satisfaction) model for facilitating motivation (Keller, 1983) were achieved. Quantitative measures indicate that students have gained new knowledge through this programme and that they appear to recognise this. Students have demonstrated a willingness to engage with this pedagogic intervention and prefer it to other modes of learning (particularly lectures) and their interview responses – evidenced above – support this view.

A new process for online social network learning in Blackboard

In view of the changes and improvements made to the online social network learning process during delivery it is suggested that a revised process has emerged, which is shown in Figure 3.5.

Recent developments using the revised online social network learning model

The revised online social network learning model was rolled out to the whole of the student cohort enrolled on the ELICS

Figure 3.5 Revised process of online social network learning

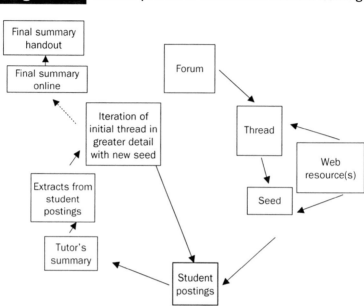

module (now entitled Research and Professional Development) in Semester 1 of 2007. A training session was held for academic colleagues in early September 2007. Once fully embedded it is hoped that this model can be used for other subjects within the university in the near future.

The activity for this year centred on students being tasked to peer review essay drafts for an assignment. Three years of very rich data has now been gathered which will be analysed and then form the basis of further published research. In the meantime, initial comments from tutors and students point towards a very positive outcome. When undertaking the online activity tutors have described students as 'engaged' and 'motivated', with large numbers of postings (30 plus) made by each seminar group. There were seven seminar groups with 12 to 15 students in each.

Early indications from data gathered from the City of Sunderland College (which at the time of writing was piloting the online social network learning process in Blackboard with A-level sociology students) appears to suggest that this process can be used in a further education environment.

A discussion board activity (following the revised online social network learning model set out above) was set up for AS sociology students during the week of 'stepping up' in the summer term of 2007. ('Stepping up' is a transition period at the end of Year 1 when students begin to address some areas of the curriculum in readiness for Year 2 in their A-level studies.) The aim was to assess how useful the discussion board environment is as a means of independent learning and for student interaction. In this short programme students were presented with an initial task of investigating the UK education system that existed before the comprehensive system. They were given the option of taking the Eleven Plus test online to get a sense of being a part of this system, and given a series of questions to discuss together online. Students were paired according to their friendship groups to enable them to feel more comfortable in this new learning environment. One half of the class attended this initial session.

The tutor reported that:

> The students took to the task very well indeed. They were very keen to participate and found the environment of the discussion board easy to use and very accessible.

However, some issues did arise:

> This initial activity brought to light some potential problems in that if a student is given a web site to look at and discuss there is a danger that they could just cut and paste.

As a result the instructions were adjusted before the second half of the group was given the task in the next session.

The students taking part in the pilot produced their own set of 'netiquette' rules, which were posted up in their classroom. It was important that the rules appeared in hard-copy and on Blackboard so that all activities had the same baseline rules.

The second half of the group worked well in the online setting:

> All students made a number of sensible contributions demonstrating a good understanding of the topic under investigation and engagement in the online discourse.

The class tutor also noted a number of positive outcomes:

> The discussion board activities did prove to be a good means of independent learning because the students have a good background knowledge on the tripartite system. This is important because it is where the A2 syllabus begins. These students will be better informed than students in previous years. The students appeared to be keen to work on the tasks that they were given and value the activities.

The class tutor noted how her role may change in this setting:

> The learning of the student also depends upon the contributions made by the lecturer; initially these were difficult to make and time consuming but it could be argued that in time this will become much easier.

The pilot appeared to be successful in a number of ways:

> It is a good means of monitoring student activity. During the period of 'independent learning' the lecturer is provided with a clear record of student activity and understanding, sound information for contributing to progress reviews.

With one problem regarding initial contributions, the online social network learning activities seemed to work well particularly for those students who are sometimes reluctant to contribute in face-to-face group working:

> It proved to be a very good environment for student interaction. In the past this activity took place in the classroom only, students entering into a discussion after doing some initial reading. With the discussion board activity every student made a contribution and joined in the activity, whereas classroom discussions can allow quiet students to say very little. Students that normally say very little contributed much more to the discussion board. The effect of this was to improve their confidence in this environment, but it is also hoped within the classroom environment too. Some student interaction was initially juvenile but this was soon addressed and a productive online discourse ensued.

Finally, the class tutor was very upbeat about online social network learning and noted several positive benefits. She also noted that this mode of working initially requires more time:

> This was most definitely a worth while exercise as it allowed the teacher to assess the level of student

interest and capability in the discussion board learning environment. The student transition into second year will prove to be much smoother than in the past. The teacher is well informed on how to produce tasks for the discussion board and has a realistic idea of how much work is involved in the monitoring of student progress in managing these activities.

Online social network learning: the e-learning holy grail?

Given that this process has translated well into different contexts it is suggested that this model provides us with a generic online discourse process, which can be used to manage this kind of activity in other Web 2.0 applications such as blogs or similar online social networked environments. It appears that the labels used here (and derived from Blackboard) for each part of the process are commonly used in some social networking applications such as MySpace. For instance, 'forum', 'thread' and 'posting' appear to be common terms, but the term 'seed' may be better understood as 'topic' in this context. Finally, the tutor would in effect be the 'topic starter' or similar depending on the setting. Whatever the context the challenge is to follow the processes described above: that learners are set a problem to be solved with appropriate resources, which provide opportunities for guided discourse, leading to a deeper understanding of a topic and ultimately to a solution – a successfully completed assignment.

Conclusion

It can be seen that online discourse particularly in the form of online social network learning engages students in successful learning. It is because student participants proved remarkably articulate and honest in the pilot and main studies that such a rich picture of online discourse and its implications could be revealed. The outcome of the main study was far more positive than the outcome of the pilot study; however, it is clear that some aspects of the programme require further work, particularly in the area of reflective practice. Although it is recognised that the findings from this study may not be generalisable to other situations and levels of new developments within ELICS (now called Research and Professional Development), the City of Sunderland College experience is encouraging. In addition, at the time of going to press, Kingston University is in the process of replicating the research described here.

In completing the online social network learning activities described here students readily demonstrated an ability to take control of the process and become active producers of knowledge rather than passive information consumers. Perhaps this is unsurprising as online social network learning replicates, albeit in an educational context, some of Web 2.0 technology's social networking aspects. By the same token tutors, while structuring and guiding discourse, became guides in facilitating the process rather than governing it. It is clear that new tutors may require additional training, particularly in managing discourse and constructing summaries.

Students appear to develop a set of robust critical thinking skills and become information sceptics, enabling them to engage effectively with the information world, which we contend is a baseline requirement for those who participate in the Web 2.0 information revolution. Hence, it is proposed that online social network learning facilitates some important processes involved in thinking, such as motivation, reflection and ultimately changed behaviour, which enables deep learning to take place. It would appear that online social networked learning may indeed be the e-learning holy grail.

The next step in this research is to migrate this generic protocol in a Web 2.0 application such as a blog in MySpace, Facebook, Beebo, Elgg or one of the plethora of new social networking tools that will undoubtedly emerge, and continue to emerge, to test to what extent online social network learning translates to online environments beyond Blackboard and indeed the university or college campus.

References

Alpay, E. (2005) Group dynamic processes in email groups, *Active Learning in Higher Education*, 6 (1), 7–16.

American Library Association (1989) *Presidential Committee on Information Literacy: final report*, *http://www.ala.org/ala/acrl/ acrlpubs/whitepapers/presidential.htm* (accessed 13 January 2004).

Andretta, S. (2005) *Information Literacy: a practitioner's guide*. Oxford: Chandos.

Big Blue Project (2002) *The Big Blue: information skills for students: final report*, *http://www.library.mmu.ac.uk/bigblue/pdf/ finalreportful.pdf* (accessed 14 January 2007).

Bordinaro, V. and Richardson, G. (2004) Scaffolding and reflection in course-integrated library instruction, *Journal of Academic Librarianship*, 30 (5), 391–401.

Brower, S. and Hollister, C. V. (2007) An interview with Patricia Senn Breivik, *Communications in Information Literacy*, 1 (1), 3–5.

Bryman, A. (2004) *Social Research Methods*, 2nd ed. Oxford: Oxford University Press.

Bundy, A. (2004) *Australian and New Zealand Information Literacy Framework: principles, standards and practice.* Adelaide: Australian and New Zealand Institute for Information Literacy, *http://www.anziil.org/resources/Info%20lit%202nd%20 edition.pdf* (accessed 8 February 2005).

CELEX (2009) *Higher Education in a Web 2.0 World: report of an independent inquiry into the impact on higher education of students' widespread use of Web 2.0 technologies*, Committee of Inquiry into the Changing Learner Experience, *http://www.jisc.ac.uk/media/documents/publications/heweb20r ptv1.pdf* (accessed 27 October 2009).

Cowan, J. (2002) *Facilitating Development Through Varieties of Reflection*. York: Higher Education Academy.

Ford, N. (2004) Towards a model of learning for educational informatics, *Journal of Documentation*, 60 (2), 183–225.

Goodyear, P. (2001) *Effective Networked Learning in Higher Education: notes and guidelines*, vol. 3 of the final report to the JISC Committee for Awareness Liaison and Training. Lancaster: Lancaster University, Centre for Studies in Advanced Learning Technology, *http://c.salt.lancs.ac.uk/JISC/guidelines_final.doc* (accessed 14 February 2005).

Hampton-Reeves, S., Mashiter, C., Westaway, J., Lumsden, P., Day, H., Hewertson, H. and Hart, A. (2009) *Students' Use of Research Content in Teaching and Learning: a report for the Joint Information Systems Council (JISC)*. Preston: University of Central Lancashire, *http://www.jisc.ac.uk/media/documents/aboutus/workinggroups/studentsuseresearchcontent.pdf* (accessed 27 October 2009).

Head, A. J. and Eisenberg, M. B. (2009) *Finding Context: what today's students say about conducting research in the digital age*. Washington, DC: University of Washington, *http://projectinfolit.org/pdfs/PIL_ProgressReport_2_2009.pdf* (accessed 27 October 2009).

Hepworth, M. (2004) A framework for understanding user requirements for an information service: defining the needs of informal carers, *Journal of the American Society of Information Science and Technology*, 55 (8), 695–708.

Hepworth, M. and Walton, G. (2009) *Teaching Information Literacy for Inquiry-based Learning*. Oxford: Chandos.

Hinett, K. (2002) *Improving Learning Through Reflection*, Part 1. York: Higher Education Academy.

Huberman, A. M. and Miles, M. B. (1994) *Data Management and Analysis Methods*. In N. K. Denzin and Y. S. Lincoln (eds) *Handbook of Qualitative Research*. Thousand Oaks, CA: Sage.

Hung, D. W. L. and Chen, D. (2001) Situated cognition, Vygotskian thought and learning from the communities of practice perspective: implications for the design of web-based e-learning, *Education Media International*, 38 (1), 3–12.

JISC infoNet (2004) Introduction to VLEs, *http://www.jiscinfonet .ac.uk/InfoKits/effective-use-of-VLEs/intro-to-VLEs/index_ html* (accessed 5 February 2010).

Keller, J. M. (1983) *Development and Use of the ARCS Model of Motivational Design*, Report IR 014 039. Enschede, Netherlands: Twente University of Technology.

Laurillard, D. (2002) *Rethinking University Teaching*. London: Routledge.

Littlejohn, A. and Higgison, C. A. (2003) *A Guide for Teachers*, E-learning Series 3. York: LTSN Generic Centre, *http:/www .ltsn.ac.uk/application.asp?app=resources.asp&process=full_ record&ion=generic&id=323* (accessed 23 March 2005).

Mayes, J. T. (1995) *Learning Technology and Groundhog Day*. In W. Strang, V. B. Simpson and J. Slater (eds) *Hypermedia at Work: practice and theory in higher education*. Canterbury: University of Kent Press.

Mayes, T. and de Freitas, S. (2004) *JISC E-learning Models Desk Study: stage 2: review of e-learning theories, frameworks and models (issue 1)*, *http://www.cetis.ac.uk:8080/pedagogy/elearning_ models/finalreportv1/* (accessed 8 February 2005).

Moseley, D., Baumfield, V., Higgins, S., Lin, M., Miller, J., Newton, D., Robson, S., Elliot, J. and Gregson, M. (2004) *Thinking Skills Frameworks for Post-16 Learners: an evaluation: a research report for the Learning & Skills Research Centre*. Trowbridge: Cromwell Press.

Nicol, D. J., Minty, I. and Sinclair, C. (2003) The social dimensions of online learning, *Innovations in Education and Teaching International*, 40 (3), 270–80.

Pope, A. and Walton, G. (2009) Information and media literacies: sharpening our vision in the twenty first century. In M. Leaning (ed.) *Issues in Information and Media Literacy: education, practice and pedagogy*. [Santa Rosa], CA: Informing Science Press, 1–29.

Race, P. (2001) *The Lecturer's Tool Kit: a resource for developing learning, teaching and assessment*, 2nd ed. London: Kogan Page.

Robson, C. (2002) *Real World Research*, 2nd ed. Oxford: Blackwell Publishing.

SCONUL (1999) *Information Skills in Higher Education: a SCONUL position paper*, Advisory Committee on Information Literacy, Society of College, National and University Libraries, *http://www.sconul.ac.uk/groups/information_literacy/papers/ Seven_pillars2.pdf* (accessed 14 January 2007).

SCONUL (2004) *Learning Outcomes and Information Literacy*. York: Higher Education Academy.

Teles, L. (1993) Cognitive apprenticeships on global networks. In L. M. Harisam, *Global Networks: computers and international communication*. Cambridge, MA: MIT Press, 271–81.

UCL (2008) *Information Behaviour of the Researcher of the Future: a CIBER briefing paper, executive summary*, University College London, *http://www.ucl.ac.uk/slais/research/ciber/ downloads/ggexecutive.pdf* (accessed 19 March 2008).

Walker, M. (2003) *Lessons in E-learning*. York: Higher Education Academy.

Walton, G., Barker, J., Hepworth, M. and Stephens, D. (2007a) Using online collaborative learning to enhance information literacy delivery in a level 1 module: an evaluation, *Journal of Information Literacy*, 1 (1), 13–30.

Walton, G., Barker, J., Hepworth, M. and Stephens, D. (2007b) Facilitating information literacy teaching and learning in a level 1 sport and exercise module by means of collaborative online and reflective learning. In S. Andretta (ed.) *Change and Challenge: information literacy for the 21st century*. Adelaide: Auslib Press.

Webb, E., Jones, A., Barker, P. and van Schaik, P. (2004) Using e-learning dialogues in higher education, *Innovations in Education and Teaching International*, 41 (1), 93–103.

Williams, P. and Rowlands, I. (2006) *Information Behaviour of the Researcher of the Future*, *http://www.jisc.ac.uk/media/documents/ programmes/reppres/ggworkpackageii.pdf* (accessed 10 June 2009).

4

E-learning models: a Web 2.0 approach to staff development in higher education

Jenny Yorke and Helen Walmsley

This chapter is written at a time of change and strong tensions within higher education. For the past decade, the introduction of e-learning and ICT more generally have been central to that change (see, for example, Bates 2000) and have served to highlight, if not aggravate, some of the tensions. It seems clear that Web 2.0 technologies, in addition to the opportunity for sharing knowledge that they promise, will provide fresh challenges. Here, we describe an approach to facilitating the uptake and quality of e-learning which uses characteristic Web 2.0 features and tools to help resolve some of the historical tensions surrounding e-learning. The approach is based on a highly participative community-of-practice model in which e-learning experts, novices and practitioners come together in the co-creation of sharable e-learning models of best practice.

Before turning to describe the approach, we briefly explore the contextual factors that inspired it. Online learning in higher education is at a curious cusp. As a surge of Web 2.0 tools is available, the long tail of academia is still trying to get grips with online learning characterised by monolithic virtual learning environments and many seem unaware of these emerging technologies and their potential impact. This is perhaps characteristic of a broader and underlying problem relating to the ability to change discussed by Shurville and Brown (2006). At a time when higher education is regarded as key to supporting the knowledge-based economies of the new century, there is some irony in the fact that, though specialising in developing and imparting knowledge, the sector seems to lack the agility necessary to transform in order to meet the challenge.

The reasons for this immobility are complex, but two are significant here. The first relates directly to libraries or information services in relation to the culture of academia. According to Becher and Trowler (2001) higher education is typified by a 'tribes and territories' culture which, Shurville and Brown (2006, 245) suggest, is manifested in a 'cultural chasm between academic staff and academic-related staff'. However, it should be noted that this is clearly not the case at Staffordshire University. Geoff Walton's work (Chapter 3) demonstrates how proactive faculty–service collaboration can lead to pedagogical innovation and shows how to circumvent some of the barriers discussed here. A second reason for the lack of agility stems from the tension between innovation and perceptions of control (Stiles and Yorke, 2006) and there seems to be a culture of resistance to strategic change, which stifles the embedding of innovation. Although many are eager to experiment with new learning and teaching technologies, the changes at an institutional level necessary to embed the technologies are often viewed as overly controlling. A contributory factor is the current context for staff development whose salient feature is the quality enhancement of teaching and learning through formalised, often imposed, professional development courses (Nicholls, 2001).

The 'eLearning Models' project was launched at Staffordshire University by the authors in May 2006 as one of a number of initiatives aimed at loosening some of the perceived bonds (Stiles and Yorke, 2006) as well as enhancing the quality and agility of e-learning development at the university. Early objectives for the project included the development of representations of approaches to e-learning which modelled good practice and, it was hoped, would guide the adoption of e-learning by novices and more experienced practitioners alike.

Best practice models

What is a best practice model? Finding a useful representation of practice is difficult because the vocabulary that individual practitioners use to describe designing and delivering e-learning is often different from each other, and the process that practitioners use to develop e-learning is often unique to the individual. The MoD4L project investigated issues of sharing and reuse of learning designs and found that 'An effective representation for sharing and reuse has not, so far, been developed, even in Further Education where sharing and reuse are institutional norms' (Falconer, 2007). We designed two different types of best practice model to explore the style that would be most useful for practitioners.

A design pattern approach was first developed and presented to practitioners. As developed by Alexander (1979), a design pattern describes a context, a problem and a 'solution' based on theory and practice, and typically includes the following characteristics:

- a name for the pattern
- a description of a problem

- the context
- the forces that play a role in coming to a solution
- the solution itself (E-LEN, [2004]).

The advantage of design patterns is that they can be seen as a sufficiently generic solution to aid ease of use in any situation or context. A design pattern was therefore developed as a guide for planning online discussions. However, the design pattern emphasis on being a solution to a 'problem' proved challenging – what is the 'problem' that an online discussion is trying to resolve? In addition, the 'design pattern' framework was seen as 'getting in the way' of the guide to planning online discussion. After discussion with practitioners, this approach was abandoned in favour of a simpler, more transparent 'activity model' that included simply a structure for an online activity.

These activity models needed to have immediacy, clarity and focus but to contain enough information to be useful. They needed to convey an easy entry point to designing an online activity that is also perceived as the 'right' way. Some new activity models were then developed from existing research-based material, for example, Salmon's five-stage model (2004) and Mayer's multimedia principles (Mayer, 2001). These models were then presented in a one-page PowerPoint slide designed to be the most simple and accessible format for users. Even in this format, some models were seen as more accessible than others. For example, Salmon's model uses simple language for each stage, but Mayer's model uses more complex language (for example, the spatial contiguity principle and the coherence principle) and despite the content being straightforward and clear otherwise, it is seen as a more difficult model.

Jones and Asensio (2002) argue that 'design for learning' requires the ability to be 'critically reflective about practice';

therefore any staff development activity needs to include the opportunity for ongoing reflection. This is because delivering e-learning activities is a process in which problems are frequently encountered and need modification and alteration. Therefore it was decided to create models that were starting points for reflection and discussion for practitioners and that enabled these discussions and reflections to be made within a community that was supportive, inclusive and striving to design the best possible e-learning. A best practice model can therefore be defined as a 'shareable model of practice' (Goodyear, 1997).

Creating a community

'Communities of practice are groups of people who share a concern, a set of problems, or a passion about a topic, and who deepen their knowledge and expertise in this area by interacting on an ongoing basis' (Wenger, 2002). They can be defined along three dimensions:

- *what it is about*: a joint enterprise as understood and continually renegotiated by its members
- *how it functions*: mutual engagement that binds members together into a social entity
- *what capability it has produced*: the shared repertoire of communal resources (routines, sensibilities, artefacts, vocabulary, styles, etc.) that members have developed over time (Smith, 2003).

Our intention was to engage e-learning practitioners in a joint enterprise (to develop e-learning skills), to create a social entity to support novice and expert practitioners alike, and to create a shared space for sharing communal resources (the best practice models). This was different from presenting them with models of best practice and hoping that they would be used as in the 'build it and they will come' model of staff development. Staff development is all too often a case of 'giving' staff information about the use of technology in teaching and learning without exemplifying the social constructivist principles that we want to encourage them to use. Beetham suggests that many e-learning practitioners have learnt to use technology through 'peer supported experimentation' and that they may well be keen to use communities of practice (Beetham, 2002). The community of practice has therefore been designed to harness collective intelligence, enable egalitarian participation and use social networking as tools to enable the community to create, share and develop the best practice models for e-learning.

There are communities of e-learning practitioners in existence (the most successful is probably the further education ILT champions JISC e-mail list, whose members share knowledge, resources and solve problems, but there is little focus on structured activity leading to a shared outcome. These champions were funded to support teachers developing e-learning in colleges of further education in the UK.) This project aimed to harness the collective intelligence of a wide range of practitioners in such a way that we would produce the shared best practice models. All activity in the best practice models for e-learning online community (*http://crusldi1.staffs.ac.uk/moodle*) is open to all members, but some activities are led by 'experts' in the 'Ask the Experts' online sessions. These are practitioners with high levels of experience and expertise (often published) who have offered to share their extensive skills with the members in the online events. This ensures that discussions are based around sound theory and relevant experience.

The online community of practice to support the best practice models project has been designed to exploit many features of Web 2.0 as both an exploration of the possibilities of the 'participatory web' and an exemplar of good practice. Web 2.0 can be seen as an attitude of egalitarian participation and shared construction of content and process. There is often a focus on participation, sharing and community for entertainment and learning. 'Here's my take on it: Web 2.0 is an attitude not a technology' (Davis, 2005).

Harness collective intelligence

The strength of communities of practice is their potential to harness collective intelligence, of which the most famous example is Wikipedia (*http://wikipedia.org*). Members are enabled, in a similar way to Wikipedia, to add content, discuss content, rate content and use core data in an innovative way. E-learning practitioners are often 'crossing borders' between their roles as teachers and technology experts. They are often innovators and may be working in isolation in their team or organisation. All those practitioners who are willing to share their experience and expertise of using e-learning are invited to join the community. Their shared domain of interest is in implementing e-learning in their institution. New members of the Best Practice Community are invited via a range of existing networks – the FE ILT Champions list, JISC, regional support centres and so on (regional support centres are funded through JISC to advise and support the use of e-learning in colleges). The Best Practice Community has members worldwide – there are currently 740+ members, mostly from the UK, but many from the USA, Australia and Asia. This has enabled a rich range of experience and expertise to be shared.

The content of the Best Practice Community site consists of models and associated resources for a range of e-learning activities, for example, online discussion, online collaboration and online case studies. The activity topics were selected to appeal to tutors as likely e-learning activities. Each of the topics has been structured in four parts:

- a research-based model presented in easily adopted format (PowerPoint presentation)

- sample case studies of the practice (links and contributed case studies)

- a selection of 'how-to' guides (for a range of tools, not just in-house ones)

- an online discussion forum for practitioners to share experience of practice.

Members can discuss content in the discussion forums created for each topic area, respond to existing topics, and participate in discussions during events. Users can rate models and see the ratings given by others. Most content is added by the project leader: the best practice models, links to selected case studies, links to tutorials and so on. However, several users have contributed case studies based on their experience and user discussions on e-learning topics are retained for reference. The core data already exists elsewhere – the models are in published literature, case studies and tutorials, largely available on the internet. Hence, the project has gathered them together in e-learning 'topics' for review by the community members in an innovative, coherent and structured way. The shared expertise and experience of this wide and varied community has become available to all. The possibilities of harnessing this collective intelligence are many, and recent developments include a small number of projects that have been instigated by members in creating new types of content to share, for example the Ecto project (*http://www.ectolearning.com*) and the 'Benefits of using a

VLE' wiki (see below for more) produced by contributors after a very lively forum discussion.

Egalitarian participation

The community is a place where members interact and learn together. In this community, a range of different activities has been planned and members have participated in many different ways. It is often assumed that Web 2.0 participation is common, that everyone can and will contribute, for example, in a similar way to Wikipedia. However, the number of folk actually contributing to Web 2.0 is generally very low. For example, the *Wall Street Journal* reports: 'At Digg, which has 900,000 registered users, 30 people were responsible for submitting one-third of postings on the home page' (Warren and Jurgensen, 2007). And McAfee states that

> In November of 2005, the most recent month for which comprehensive stats are available, Wikipedia had over 850,000 articles in English, and 2.9 million across all languages (including more than 10,000 in Esperanto). This content was generated by fewer than 50,000 contributors in English, and 103,000 [in] total.
>
> McAfee, 2006

Many online communities, like Digg and Wikipedia, seem to have a high level of 'non-participants' or 'lurkers' and this is true of the Best Practice Community. A recent survey and anecdotal evidence suggests that although the participants value the resources and are interested in the ongoing discussions, they contact other members directly to discuss topics further or they follow up links and resources without always feeding back to the group. Lave and Wenger (1991) argue that learning 'is a process of participation in communities of practice, participation that is at first legitimately peripheral but that increases gradually in engagement and complexity'. Therefore, many of the Best Practice Community activities are specifically designed to actively interest and engage participation and to draw members gradually into the centre of the community, rather than waiting for it to occur.

The best practice model for an e-learning online community has run a wide range of face-to-face and online activities to encourage staff to participate in the community. The following account demonstrates that some activities are more likely to lead to staff participation in creation and development than others.

In October 2006, an event, 'Collaborating on elearning models', was set up to introduce staff to the existing models and to run an activity to engage them in discussion about their e-learning practice. It was intended that there would be additions to the models as an outcome of the event, but the staff felt unsure about adding to an existing model; however, they contributed items for discussion, for example:

> The following is an initial list of 'areas' considered to be relevant to engagement – have any been missed off this list? Is this on the right lines; are there any other issues that have been overlooked?
>
> ■ Discussion guidelines are necessary for effective engagement.
>
> ■ Tutors need to decide on discussion 'mix' at outset (asynchronous reflection?) versus synchronous (immediacy of engagement?).
>
> How complete is this initial list?
>
> John Erskine, community member

A different activity, 'Comparing models of good practice', asked participants to review an existing model and a sample case study describing the e-learning activity in use. The participants were able to compare the extent to which the case study matched the model, but were then able to see that the model could be used to compare with their own practice. This seems to create a sense of distance from the model that allows practitioners to use it without feeling that it is too restrictive. For example, one participant commented:

> It motivated me to critically analyse the case studies – thus developing my ability to critically analyse my own practise.

> Anonymous

In the 'Ask the experts' sessions, members ('experts') with experience of the topic were invited to present their case studies. During the session, members were able to ask open or unstructured questions to the 'experts' and to each other. This simple model of an online workshop has enabled members with very different levels of skill and experience to learn from and connect with each other.

Later activities with shared outcomes, which we call 'topic workshops', have been more successful in engaging practitioners with creating material. Indeed, these have sometimes been instigated by members, as in the discussion about potential uses for Second Life in education. A member of the community raised the topic in the forum, and another member volunteered to run a live demonstration at the university. As a result, a wiki with the discussion outcomes was created to contribute to the community. In addition, a workshop on the use of Skype using a Google docs page to collate contributions was delivered in response to questions about the use of the tool. After the event, a volunteer from the group adapted the discussions and ideas into a short guide to using Skype for teaching, which was then posted back to the community. The range of innovative suggestions suggested that the participants were considering new uses for Skype and not just enhancing existing practice. For example, they suggested that Skype could be used for:

- ice breaking activities in advance of more organised group work to enable students and tutors to develop a social presence

- students' peer discussion (recorded) to reflect on as a learning article

- a formal Q&A session between tutor and student as part of assessment

- individual presentations by students to groups of students or to tutors

- providing feedback about assessments

- drama, play reading, role playing, debates; use images and icons to represent different characters, roles or teams

- groups reviewing or commenting on resources and activities

- collaboration between students and peer-support.

As the community has become more mature, other projects have emerged that do not rely on the 'seeding' of the community co-ordinator. For example, a recent discussion on the benefits of using a VLE started in one of the forums. This developed into a very extensive discussion with over 40 posts in a few days. The instigator and another volunteer agreed to summarise and organise the discussion into a wiki page. This is now available to the community as a valuable resource and is still being edited. The editor of the wiki said:

> I found working on the recent Wiki on 'Benefits of a VLE' interesting and informative. I had never contributed to one before so I can now add this to my CV! After all, isn't this e-learning thing all about social collaboration? I thought that my post precipitated the very best of this – people posted in many ideas, thoughts and experiences that I would never have got from anywhere else. The phrase 'social collaboration' seemed an empty one before this!
>
> Tony Bilny, community member

To continue the range of opportunities for egalitarian participation wikis have been created for the online discussions topic in the community to allow participants to add their own comments and ideas for activities.

Social networking

Finally, the use of Web 2.0 social networking tools such as Facebook and Ning has been explored to see what it could offer to the community. A review of these tools and the current community created in Moodle showed that:

- There are a large number of asynchronous discussion forums in the Best Practice Community, but no way to see easily what was new, or who was contributing. The forums are set to send an e-mail copy to all members automatically and many members simply read the postings (or filed them) without logging on.

- Facebook and Ning show 'social exhaust' – list postings, comments and contributions – as current activity. The Moodle community has no way to show that anything was happening. It made the site look like a flat website full of resources.

- Editable personal profiles are available in the community, but they are not easily visible and it is not possible to create networks of friends, or to see the friends of your friends. Facebook makes it easy to add friends with common interests and to see the networks around them. Ning also allows you to create networks within the community, and to see friends and networks of your friends, but you can't add them as your friend, and you can't easily join other people's networks.

- The community has a facility for sending messages, but these don't always work, and there is no message centre to see sent, new and saved messages. Facebook allows you to comment on a friend's page, add a message to a 'wall' or to send a private message. Ning allows similar features.

Ning has now been set up as a separate 'open' network to provide a social networking space for the Best Practice Community – non-members can join. There are forums, videos and RSS feeds from some of the main discussions on the best practice site and there are currently 155 members of this network. The Best Practice Community now has a link to the Ning network (with an attractive image!) and RSS feeds show the recent activity.

This new network has encouraged new members to participate. There have been several postings about the use of Ning on the Ning forums from community members who had previously been only 'lurking':

I already have a Ning account so thought I'd come along for the ride... I enjoyed reading and taking part in the various Best Practice discussions this week through the Moodle forums.

Clare McCullagh, Ning member

I too have a Ning account and several different networks that I have created or am participating in. I am very interested in the power of such tools and perhaps this may make me more active here than I was in Moodle.

Debra Marsh, Ning member

Yes it is interesting that people tend to prefer contributing to social sites. I am currently involved in a number of different initiatives both here in France and back in the UK involving social networks on Ning. The aims and expected outcomes of these initiatives are all quite different but there is one common feature emerging and that is that interaction between the participants is much more active and engaged on the Ning Social Networks than on the established VLEs of the different institutions (i.e. Web CT, Blackboard, Moodle, Sakai).

Debra Marsh, Ning member

I've been following the lively recent discussions and, as ever, learning much from them. Oddly, I was thinking these discussions would be great in a Ning site or in the wider community at Classroom 2.0 when I noticed you have set up this network. Is there now a need for the Moodle space? What might be criteria for deciding where to post?

Pete Whitfield, Ning member

In summary, the project aimed to facilitate the creation and use of best practice models of e-learning by practitioners. An online community of practice using some Web 2.0 style tools was created and a range of activities planned and delivered. The community has enabled much harnessing of collective intelligence, egalitarian participation and the growing use of social networking. The models are not fixed templates for practitioners to 'use', but fluid starting points that can be shared together with our experience of using them.

A model for developing models of best practice has therefore emerged through the community of practice (Figure 4.1). Practitioners review the models provided in the community; then compare them to case studies of e-learning in their own and others' practice in formal and informal community activities; finally they contribute their own discussion, summary or case study to inform the use of the model in practice.

Figure 4.1   Developing models of best practice

Best practice model taken from research

Compare model to case or own experience in community event

Produce summary or wiki to inform use of model in practice

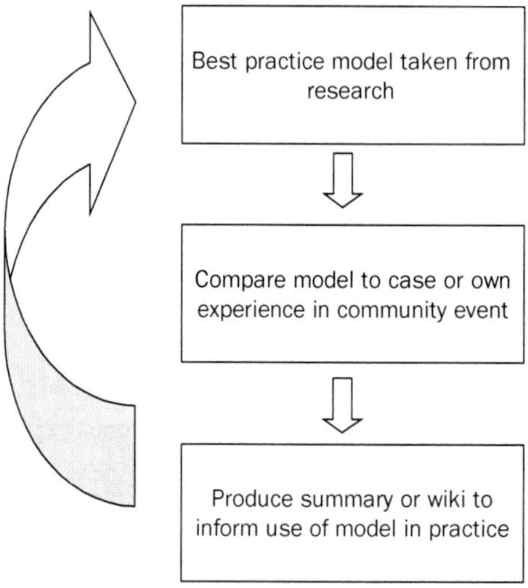

Discussion

Quality: shifting the locus of ownership

Many universities have been quick to spot the practical merits of e-learning, such as enhancing the flexibility of time and place of study and helping to reach new, often global, markets. However, these expectations have been accompanied by deep concern over whether technology will be used in a way that enhances the quality of learning (e.g. Mayes, 1995, or Stiles, 2004). This, coupled with a tradition in approaches to quality in higher education towards monitoring and control, can lead institutions to adopt rather onerous and unpopular processes to assure the quality of e-learning which can stifle innovation. At Staffordshire University, the e-learning model work is central to a transformative approach to quality aimed at loosening perceived bonds of control and enabling innovation. The models are used to provide examples of good practice which academic developers can use to transform their practice as they adopt e-learning. However, combined with the supporting case studies, they provide a powerful means of enabling academic staff to interrogate both the model and their own practice. Although the models suggest approaches in which quality is inherent from the outset, the supporting case studies elucidate how it can be built into course design. Together, they provide a means of improving practice in a thoughtful way in which quality enhancement is likely to be perceived as a constructive and reflective process rather than imposed.

A deep approach to e-learning?

In assessing the importance of the strategies used by the project to share good practice in e-learning, it is useful to note that staff in higher education, faced with understanding how to use new technologies to support learning and teaching, are effectively placed in the role of student. The manner in which students approach learning and its relation to the quality of understanding has been illuminated by the research of Marton and Säljö (1997) and Entwistle (1998), which showed that students tend to take a surface or deep approach. Although we are explicit about expecting students to take a deep approach to learning and berating those who take a surface approach, it is all too common in staff development to use approaches that not only encourage a surface approach, but seem almost to impel it.

The recent ascent of 'knowledge transfer' and a focus on the efficiency of learning rather than its effectiveness may further encourage approaches to staff development along the lines of the 'Nurnberg funnel' (Carroll, 1990) model, in which learners are treated as the passive receivers of information, poured down through the 'funnel of staff development' into their awaiting 'sponge-like' brains. The tendency of such strategies to promote surface approaches is reinforced by the climate of fast-moving change in which many staff feel under time-pressure: it is our experience that time – where to find it – is one of the most frequently cited issues by those embarking on using technology to support learning.

One of the characteristics of a deep approach is the intent on the part of learners to understand rather than only to memorise (Entwistle, 1998). How to motivate this intent by designing learning environments and activities that foster a deep approach rather than inhibit it is an enduring concern among staff in higher education. Although we have found it very difficult to derive models that, when used alone, promote deep learning, it is becoming evident that the combination of strategies used as part of the e-learning models project seem to be more successful. We summarise these as follows. First, as we have noted, the case studies we provide to accompany the models seem to be used by practitioners to reflect on the model, to interrogate it or to shed more light on it. The 'Ask the experts' sessions allow practitioners to develop their understanding of models and improve the quality of their own technology-supported learning through verbal question and answer sessions around the use of a particular model. Both these methods are seen as helping to promote a deeper understanding of a model in order to apply it. Other strategies we use, principally to help share good practice, encourage a deep approach in other ways. For example, during the 'Sharing good practice in e-learning' seminars, we ask practitioners already established in using e-learning to share their approach with novice practitioners by comparing it with one of 'best practice models'. This encourages the established practitioners to reflect on their own approach as well as engage them with other approaches. The depth of critical reflection evidenced – the models seem to enable practitioners to critique their own approach – and its success in engaging novice practitioners has been one of the most revelatory successes of the project.

Formal staff development strategies

In addition to the strategies towards 'informal' staff development described above, e-learning models have also been embedded into formal, accredited, postgraduate-level staff development opportunities (Stiles and Yorke, 2006). The intention with which models are used here is opposite to that described above where they were seen primarily as a way of helping practitioners focus on the practical aspects of using e-learning to understand underlying quality issues and pedagogic theory. In the formal staff development opportunities, models are used primarily to help practitioners make links between theories of learning and teaching and e-learning practice, to help them understand how to put theory into practice.

Bridging chasms

The ability for non-academic staff to engage academic staff and to communicate with them meaningfully across their institution is imperative if technological developments are to lend and develop the agility sought of them. At Staffordshire University we are using the e-learning models work as a significant way of enabling learning technologists to develop meaningful discourse with academic staff in the design and development of e-learning, which goes well beyond the topic of 'how to use the technology' that such discourse often covers.

Models can act effectively as conceptual frameworks for approaches to e-learning and at the same time act as 'bridges' between practice and theory. As conceptual frameworks, they can provide a means of enabling academic and non-academic staff to develop a shared language and understanding of approaches to e-learning, although as we have discussed this process needs to be augmented with other resources, such as case studies. As 'bridges', models allow 'tribes' to gain deeper insight into the theoretical underpinnings of those approaches and to discuss them in both practical and more theoretical terms. Models also provide a means for comparing different approaches to e-learning which, together with the greater theoretical understanding they foster, can enable discussion about the appropriateness of different models for different educational contexts or aims in a critical and objective way. Used in this way they provide an approach to staff development which is exploratory rather than prescriptive.

Conclusion

We end this chapter by commenting on some important issues highlighted by the e-learning models project. First, we have suggested models can be thought of as representations of practice. However, finding an adequate way of representing practice has proved extremely difficult. That said, some of the characteristics of good representations are becoming clear. These include simplicity and accessibility. It is important that neither jargon nor the framework itself act as barriers to initial engagement. The framework needs to be self-evident – as in Gilly Salmon's five-stage model (2004) – or transparent. It is also vitally important that the model seems to make sense so that it engages at a 'practice level'. Most importantly, if they are to be taken seriously, models need to be based on sound evidence of what works and on credible theories of learning and teaching.

Despite the difficulty of finding adequate representations, the e-learning models project has clearly demonstrated the power models have in attracting and engaging practitioners and in building a community of practice. However, as we have stressed, models need to be augmented by other strategies to enable them to be useful beyond that initial revelation of 'common sense', and at a level that enables a deep understanding of how they enhance learning and teaching and can be put into practice. Diverse strategies also need to be used to keep the community vibrant and progressive and to prevent it from becoming a static resource.

Finally, there is the issue of ownership. Salient among the diverse strategies aimed at encouraging a sense of ownership of the models among individuals and the community of practice we have suggested is to see the models not as the static representation of expert practice, but as adaptable. Models are useful, as we have noted, in providing initial conceptual frameworks for people to start to engage with how e-learning might be approached, but that is also their limitation. Meaningful practice is too fluid to be captured fully by a framework and so it is important to ensure that the framework is used only so long as it is useful and does not becomes a stricture.

As we have discussed, ownership of an approach at an individual level is almost a necessary criterion for promoting reflective practice in which concerns for quality or the critical enhancement of practice can be adopted by practitioners themselves. However, important as individual ownership is, institutional ownership is crucial to ensuring that the good practice that the models endeavour to mediate is recognised and endorsed.

In our experience, it is clear that models provide a way of engaging different 'tribes' in the joint pursuit of sharing good practice in e-learning. Moreover, there is good reason to hope that, by using the additional strategies we have described and models to mediate 'expert practice', we can promote consistent good practice across the many territories which make up a university. There is good evidence to suggest that the community of practice we have established within the university is helping to provide 'horizontal coherence' (Romanainen, 2004) by providing a way of enabling novice practitioners to learn from those with greater expertise. Within the community, the models help to mediate the transition of novices from being (legitimate) peripheral observers of good practice towards being expert practitioners by providing representations of 'expert' knowledge. Importantly, they promote coherence through the consistent representation of 'expert practice'.

Although a community of practice approach may help foster horizontal coherence, this is only one step towards ensuring that good practice is embedded. Indeed, such approaches may not have the means to achieve full organisational embedding until they themselves are integrated into existing organisational processes, which can be a challenge:

> The very characteristics that make communities of practice a good fit for stewarding knowledge – autonomy, practitioner-orientation, informality, crossing boundaries – are also characteristics that make them a challenge for traditional hierarchical organizations. How this challenge is going to affect these organizations remains to be seen.

> Wenger, 2006

Stiles and Yorke (2004) discuss the importance of achieving vertical and horizontal coherence in the effective embedding of e-learning. In other words, practice, institutional policy and processes need to be in consistent harmony across the institution for embedding to be achieved. Vertical coherence is the role and realm of governance and although communities of practice may provide an informal means of establishing horizontal coherence, they can only promote institutional coherence to the extent to which the processes and practice reflect or inform institutional policy.

In our opinion institutional quality processes hold the key to ensuring that these horizontal and vertical dimensions are joined up. Thus, in the specific case of the e-learning models project, a key strand of work still in progress is the development of particular models, which will be 'exposed' to university quality processes with a view to achieving the university's endorsement of those models and embedding them into the quality processes. A secondary aim is to 'badge' certain models in the development of a 'fast track' through the quality process: basically, the idea is that course leaders who can demonstrate that their course adheres to one of the 'badged' models need not go through the more onerous process of demonstrating the validity of the approach.

References

Alexander, C. (1979) *The Timeless Way of Building*. New York: Oxford University Press.

Bates, A. W. (2000) *Managing Technological Change*. San Francisco, CA: Jossey Bass.

Becher, T. and Trowler, P. R. (2001) *Academic Tribes and Territories*. Buckingham: Society for Research into Higher Education and Oxford University Press.

Beetham, H. (2002) *Networks of Practice/Representation of Practice: a position paper on the development of innovative learning technology practice in UK HE, http://www2 .plymouth.ac.uk/ed/ELT%20documents/EFFECTS/Vision.pdf* (accessed 21 December 2009).

Carroll, J. M. (1990) *The Nurnberg Funnel: designing minimalist instruction for practical computer skill*. Cambridge, MA: MIT Press.

Davis, I. (2005) Talis, Web 2.0 and that, *Internet Alchemy*, 4 July, *http://iandavis.com/blog/2005/07/talis-web-20-and-all-that? year=2005&monthnum=07&name=talis-web-20-and-all-that*.

E-LEN [2004] *Design Expertise for E-Learning Centres: design patterns and how to produce them, http://www2.tisip.no/ E-LEN/documents/ELEN-Deliverables/booklet-e-len_design_ experience.pdf* (accessed 21 December 2009).

Entwistle, N. (1998) *Styles of Learning and Teaching: an integrated outline of educational psychology*. London: David Fulton.

Falconer, I. (2007) *Mod4L Summary Report, http://www.academy .gcal.ac.uk/mod4l/mod4lsummaryreport.doc* (accessed November 2007).

Goodyear, P. (1997) The ergonomics of learning environments: learner-managed learning and new technology, paper given at EDUTEC '97 (3rd Congress on New Information Technologies for Education), Malaga, 7–17 October. In M. C. de la Serna (ed.) *Creacion de materiales para la innovacion educativa con nuevas tecnologias*. Malaga, Spain: Instituto de Ciencias de la Educación, Universidad de Málaga, *http://www.ieev.uma .es/edutec97/edu97_co/goodyear.htm* (accessed August 2007).

Jones, C. and Asensio, M. (2002) Designs for networked learning in higher education: a phenomenographic investigation of practitioners' accounts of design. In C. Steeples and C. Jones (eds) *Networked Learning: perspectives and issues*. London: Springer-Verlag.

Lave, J. and Wenger, E. (1991) *Situated Learning: legitimate peripheral participation*. Cambridge: University of Cambridge Press.

Marton, F. and Säljö, R. (1997) Approaches to learning. In F. Marton, D. Hounsell and N. Entwistle (eds) *The Experience of Learning: implications for teaching and studying in higher education*. Edinburgh: Scottish Academic Press.

Mayer, R. (2001) *Multimedia Learning*. Cambridge, New York: Cambridge University Press.

Mayes, J. T. (1995) Learning technology and groundhog day. In W. Strang, V. B. Simpson and D. Slater (eds) *Hypermedia at Work: practice and theory in higher education*. Canterbury: University of Kent Press, *http://apu.gcal.ac.uk/clti/papers/ Groundhog.html* (accessed November 2007).

McAfee, A. (2006) Does Web 2.0 guarantee Enterprise 2.0? Andrew McAfee's blog: the business impact of IT, 15 April, *http://blog.hbs.edu/faculty/amcafee/index.php/faculty_amcafee_v3/ does_web_20_guarantee_enterprise_20/* (accessed 21 December 2009).

Nicholls, G. (2001) *Professional Development in Higher Education*. London: Kogan Page.

Romanainen, J. (2004) Technology foresight in context – shaping and aligning policies for innovation, *http://www.forfas.ie/news/ foresight_for_innovation_conference_2004/programme/5* (accessed 9 November 2006).

Salmon, G. (2004) *E-moderating: the key to teaching and learning online*. London: RoutledgeFalmer.

Shurville, S. and Browne, T. (2006) Introduction: ICT-driven change in higher education: learning from eLearning, *Journal of Organisational Transformation and Social Change*, 3 (3), 245–50.

Smith, M. K. (2003) Communities of practice. In *The Encyclopaedia of Informal Education, www.infed.org/biblio/ communities_of_practice.htm* (accessed November 2007).

Stiles, M. J. (2004) Strategic and pedagogic requirements for virtual learning in the context of widening participation. In D. S. Preston (ed.) *At the Interface: virtual learning and higher education.* Amsterdam; New York: Rodopi.

Stiles, M. and Yorke, J. (2006) Technology supported learning: tensions between innovation and control, and organisational and professional cultures, *Journal of Organisational Transformation and Social Change*, 3 (3), 251–67.

Stiles, M. J. and Yorke, J. M. E. (2004) Embedding staff development in elearning in the production process and using policy to reinforce its effectiveness, an informal discussion paper for the 9th SEDA Conference, Birmingham, November, *http://www.staffs.ac.uk/COSE/cosenew/embedding.pdf.*

Warren, J. and Jurgensen, J. (2007) The wizards of buzz, *Wall Street Journal,* 10 February, *http://online.wsj.com/public/ article/SB117106531769704150-zpK10wf4CJOB4IKoJS5anu Noi6Y_20080209.html* (accessed October 2007).

Wenger, E. (2002) *Cultivating Communities of Practice.* Boston: Harvard Business School Press.

Wenger, E. (2006) *Communities of Practice: a brief introduction, http://www.ewenger.com/theory/index.htm* (accessed 21 December 2009).

Part 3:
Technology

5

A deployment strategy for maximising the impact of institutional use of Web 2.0

Brian Kelly

Introduction

The benefits of Web 2.0 are now widely acknowledged, but before embracing use of Web 2.0 organisations need to be aware of potential risks and to develop strategies for managing such risks. This chapter illustrates how various Web 2.0 technologies (such as blogs, wikis and social networks) are becoming accepted and are being embedded within our institutions, initially perhaps by individuals and early adopters, but increasingly as part of the core services provided by the institution.

The effective exploitation of Web 2.0 will require an understanding of how such services can be used to support institutional objectives and the selection of services to support these aims. The section of externally hosted services will require an assessment not only of the functionality of the services but also of their sustainability. However, it would be a mistake to focus only on the services themselves. An important aspect of Web 2.0 are the softer characteristics, such as the view as the network as a mechanism for delivering applications, trust in users and the 'always beta' nature of web-based services. Jenny Yorke and Helen Walmsley in Chapter 4 explore how this issue might be addressed via an online community of practice for teaching staff. Geoff Walton in Chapter 3 indicates that a technologically independent e-pedagogy can mitigate the effects of 'constant beta'. David Ley in Chapter 6 explores the technological developments in more detail. Many of these aspects of Web 2.0 challenge well-established approaches to the development and deployment of IT services, where the application is managed in a stable environment, the release of updates is agreed with the user community and the trust of the user is managed by contractual obligations or agreement with institutional terms and conditions.

A number of case studies that outline the potential benefits of externally hosted Web 2.0 services are provided, together with details of the approaches that have been taken to the risk assessment of such services. These examples are used in the development of a risk assessment and risk management toolkit, which seeks to ensure that institutions have a better understanding of the risks and have document strategies in place for managing them.

Examples of uses of Web 2.0 services

In order to illustrate ways in which Web 2.0 can help to maximise impact we will consider some examples of popular Web 2.0 services.

- *Wikipedia*: Although its detractors point to the lack of formal and well-established quality assurance processes, the popularity of Wikipedia cannot be disputed. The list of libraries in Wikipedia is not as comprehensive as the list of museums, but the libraries that do have a presence in Wikipedia, such as John Rylands Library (*http://en.wikipedia.org/wiki/John_Rylands_Library*), gain benefits from the popularity of Wikipedia and the increased Google ranking to the John Rylands website provided by links from the Wikipedia website.

- *Facebook*: The University of Wolverhampton's learning centres have a Facebook presence (*http://www.facebook.com/wlvlc*), which provide links to institutional resources, embedded search facilities (such as searches of the JSTOR and COPAC services), the ability to become a 'fan' of the learning centres and a means of providing news in an environment which many students at the university are likely to use and be familiar with.

- *Blogs*: Blogs provide a simple and easy to use mechanism for alerting users to new developments within a library and soliciting feedback. At Imperial College London blogs were set up by library liaison staff initially for the physics and maths and engineering departments. Following the success of these initial experiments 13 blogs have now been established and this is felt to provide a valuable service to the user community (Evans, 2009).

- *Twitter*: Increasing numbers of librarians and information professionals use Twitter. This 'micro-blogging' service is being used for a variety of purposes, including peer support, engagement with fellow librarians and dissemination and engagement with library users. Examples of librarian Twitter users can be seen from the list of 100 British librarians on Twitter (Bradley, 2010).

Maximising the impact of Web 2.0 within an organisation

A Web 2.0 deployment strategy

In order to maximise the impact that Web 2.0 can have within an organisation it can be helpful to devise a deployment strategy that aims to exploit the enthusiasms of the early adopters, leading to embedding of Web 2.0 technologies within the organisation.

The following elements of a deployment strategy are suggested:

- advocacy
- engagement with enthusiasts and early adopters
- listening to and addressing concerns
- user education
- embedding.

The initial activities are likely to start with small-scale experimentation by early adopters. In order that the enthusiasms of the early adopters can lead to embedding of services within the institution it can be helpful for the early adopters to engage with fellow enthusiasts who might be willing to make use of emerging new technologies. Ways of structuring and harnessing the enthusiasm of adopters are illustrated in Chapter 4.

A potential danger with groups of early adopters and enthusiasts is that they fail to recognise possible apprehension that others may have. It is desirable, therefore, to listen to others within the organisation in order to understand their concerns. This activity should lead to expectation management (avoiding the inevitable over-hyping of new technologies) and strategies for addressing concerns that have been raised.

The need for education and training is clearly of importance. It should be noted that this should include providing an understanding of Web 2.0 concepts and not just training in a particular application. In addition it can be helpful if the training made use of Web 2.0 concepts, for example by using the Common Craft series of videos (*http://www.commoncraft.com/*), which introduces topics such as blogs, wikis, social networks, RSS and so on. The outcome of this deployment strategy should be the embedding of Web 2.0 services to support organisational needs.

In order for this approach to be realised there is a need to have a good understanding of what is meant by the term 'Web 2.0'. In addition it will be important to be able to identify barriers to deployment and to devise strategies for addressing them.

Web 2.0 applications

For many the term Web 2.0 is associated with applications such as blogs and wikis. A broader understanding of the term embraces services that allow users to create content and to comment on content provided by others. This encompasses various social sharing services, such as those for photographs (e.g. Flickr), videos (e.g. YouTube) and bookmarks (e.g. Delicious). The term Web 2.0 also includes web-based technologies for communicating with others. Initially the main focus of such communications services covered web-based chat facilities, which complemented instant messaging technologies such as MSN Messenger. More recently the communications aspect of Web 2.0 has focused on social networks such as Facebook and MySpace, later followed by Twitter, which provide communications between friends and mechanisms for interacting with others with similar interests. This, then, might be considered to be the users' view of Web 2.0. A developer, however, might also wish to highlight the fact that the popularity of such applications is helped by the ease of use and usability of such services provided by advances in user-interface technologies offered by tools such as Ajax or Flash-based interfaces to services. The developer might also add that provision and use of rich content in such services is provided by syndication technologies such as RSS and Atom and the provision of, often lightweight, application programming interfaces (APIs), by such Web 2.0 services.

With a slippery concept such as Web 2.0 it can be difficult to provide a simple definition that covers both users' perceptions of Web 2.0 and those of developers. However, although Web 2.0 was initially derided by sceptics as marketing hype, it is now clear that the term has gained widespread currency and that many organisations are seeking to exploit the potential of Web 2.0. To take one specific Web 2.0 application area let us look at how libraries are making use of blogs. The early adopters of blogs were, as might be expected, those in the web development community. However, particularly in the USA, the academic and library sector began to appreciate the benefits that could be gained through use of blogs in teaching and learning (e.g. to encourage reflective learning or team working) and within the library (e.g. to disseminate information using technologies that, through use of RSS, would allow the information to be easily reused by a variety of different tools or as a discussion forum to encourage feedback from the user community). These early adopters often wished to make use of blogging software before the institution was in a position to provide access to software in-house. This led the enthusiasts who were not in a position to install software simply to make use of externally hosted services such as Blogger or WordPress, which required no software to be installed locally and needed little technical expertise to set up and deploy.

In many higher educational institutions the role of blogs to support educational needs is becoming accepted. Institutions are now beginning to deploy blogging services either through the installation of blogging software locally or through blog functionality being provided in other systems, such as an enterprise virtual leaning environment (VLE).

The use of blogs within the public library sector is patchier, however. This is probably because of concerns related to some of the softer aspects of Web 2.0, such as ownership of technologies, trusting users and willingness to take risks, rather than technical issues. We will now explore these issues in more detail.

Web 2.0 culture

Tim O'Reilly's famous Web 2.0 meme map (see Figure 7.1) includes the following phrases, which aim to characterise Web 2.0: 'an attitude not a technology', 'the perpetual beta', 'the rights to remix', 'trust your users' and 'small pieces loosely connected', with Web 2.0 strategically positioned as 'The Web as Platform' (O'Reilly, 2005). It is Web 2.0 as an attitude not a technology which is challenging many institutions: the notion of services that may change without notice may be felt to undermine the expertise of support staff and can make obsolete documentation and training materials; the rights to remix can conflict with the desire of organisations to control their materials and prevent potential misuse; staff's trust in users does not appear to be able to coexist easily with the need to manage the security of networking services in order to prevent viruses, denial of service attacks, spam and so on; and the management of small, loosely connected pieces may be in conflict with institutional commitment to enterprise solutions.

Most importantly, perhaps, are the challenges provided by Web 2.0 strategically positioning itself as 'The Web as Platform'. To date the platform for delivering applications has been the computer; initially the computer was a mainframe system but in the 1980s the PC became the important platform for many users. With the growth of computer networks we reached a hybrid position in which the PC is often the platform of choice on the end users' desktop, but this is closely coupled with server systems, which could be Unix, Microsoft Windows or a combination of the two. It is this well-established environment of delivering applications through use of a variety of in-house systems that Web 2.0 is challenging. When users make use of Google to find resources, Google Mail to send e-mail to their colleagues, Flickr to share their photographs or Facebook to update their friends on their activities, none of these services are based on in-house services. And although many will use these services for personal and social purposes, increasingly institutions such as universities and colleges are starting to explore the potential of such services to support both formal and informal learning. An initial reason for this may be to enable students to make use of tools they are familiar with and will still be able to use once they have graduated. But the ease of use of many Web 2.0 services and their popularity is leading to institutions asking whether externally hosted services can be used more generally and not just for small-scale or informal teaching and learning purposes.

Two tribes

Staff in IT service departments within institutions will often see their role as providing reliable, secure and managed services for use by their user community. These goals are clearly laudable, and when services become unavailable or are unreliable the IT services department is the first to receive criticism. So it is understandable that staff in many IT service departments have concerns about relying on third party services, especially when there are no formal contracts or service level agreements.

And yet institutions, in particular those within the higher education community, may also value the flexibility to exploit innovative solutions. Innovative IT applications may be of particular interest to the research community, for use in niche areas in which there are limited developments provided by the commercial sector. But in addition to supporting their research interests, institutions may also feel that they have a responsibility to ensure that their students have encountered technologies which they may expect to use when they graduate, and that they have developed an awareness of the risks associated with use of such technologies. And finally such innovation may eventually become the mainstream solution of tomorrow, as was seen during the 1980s when the PC was perceived by many in central IT service departments as initially an irrelevance, before becoming a threat to existing structures, before eventually emerging as the main access point for many users in the institution.

We can see that there are conflicting views, which may be deeply embedded within organisational cultures. The ease of use of Web 2.0 services is bringing many of these tensions to the fore. There is a need to gain a better understanding of the concerns of these two diverse views held by the 'two tribes' (Kelly, 2007).

The managed environment

An IT environment that is hosted and managed locally has been the norm for many large organisations, especially in the higher education sector, which traditionally provides IT service departments with a responsibility for managing and supporting the IT technologies used within the institution. In this environment IT services will have well-established working practices for managing and developing the infrastructure (managing growth in usage, understanding vendors' roadmaps for developments to their software, and so on) and providing the necessary user support (such as education and training, help desk and FAQs). The working culture within this environment is well understood, with established mechanisms for managing change and development.

The outsourced environment

The term 'outsourced environment' is an emotive one within public sector organisations in the UK, with its implications of privatisation and outsourcing of public sector services. Yet wide area networks are at the heart of the delivery of services to remote organisations. This is well understood and fundamental to the role of the national services (such as Mimas and EDINA), which JISC fund on behalf of the UK's higher and further education communities. A reliance on third party services is understood by everyone who has ever used Google and, at a more technical layer, the internet itself (the network, the routers, the DNS gateways and so on) is dependent on a devolved, distributed provision of the network infrastructure.

The tensions therefore relate not to the nature of third party services *per se*, but rather to the sustainability of such services and their accompanying business models. The provision of networked services within a community of shared values and a tradition of collaboration, such as the UK higher education environment, is widely accepted. The provision of networked services by commercial companies is new, however, and leads to concerns as to whether such services are in a position to deliver sustainable services and uncertainties regarding changes to such services.

The concerns

Those with a responsibility for providing a managed secure and reliable IT infrastructure would probably raise the following concerns about the use of third party services:

- *Performance and reliability*: Will a third party service provide the satisfactory levels of performance and reliability that may be needed for use in mission-critical activities?

- *Security*: Will data held on third party service be secure? Can it be guaranteed, for example, that personal data will not be divulged to third parties?

- *Legal issues*: Will the service comply with appropriate legislation, including data protection, copyright, defamation, accessibility and so on? Will the organisation making use of third party services be liable for failures by the service to comply with legislation?

- *Accessibility and usability*: Is the service usable by people with disabilities? Who is legally responsible if the service fails to comply with accessibility legislation?

- *Sustainability*: Will the service be sustainable in the long run? If the service is not sustainable, how much notice will users be given?

- *Interoperability (data migration)*: Can data be exported from the service? How easy is it to do this? How rich and how complete will the data be? How easy will it be to import the data into a new application and rebuild a new service?

- *Interoperability (data integration)*: Is the service interoperable with other applications? Does it support relevant standards?

- *Terms and conditions*: What terms and conditions does the service define? Are such terms and conditions of concern? Can the terms and conditions change, and what would be the implication of changes?

These are the concerns that are likely to be expressed openly, and it should be acknowledged that there are also likely to be concerns that will not be openly articulated. These might include individual concerns (such as fears over job losses and deskilling) and departmental concerns (such as departmental downsizing or reductions to levels of funding).

There may be additional concerns, perhaps at a political level (such as dangers that political tensions may hinder the exchange of data such as the dispute seen in 2009 between Russia and Estonia), or at a macro-economic level (use of IT developed in other countries may undermine a local IT development industry). However, as it is difficult to predict the implications of such large-scale challenges, this chapter will focus on issues that can (and should) be addressed within the organisation.

Addressing the concerns

It would be very easy to become despondent over the lack of any guarantee of the long-term sustainability of third party Web 2.0 services. The companies will typically refuse to provide cast-iron guarantees over the long-term sustainability of their services and are likely to reserve the rights to change their terms and conditions at any time. However, it should be borne in mind that similar uncertainties also exist with Google's search facility, as there is no certainty that Google will continue to provide this service. Nevertheless, as we all know, the Google search engine has grown in popularity since it was launched and this has contributed to Google's financial success. Experiences with traditional licensed IT applications have also shown us that using licensed software and having a formal contract with a company that supports the software is no guarantee that the software is sustainable in the long run. Rather than having cast-iron guarantees or relying on using only mature services, an alternative approach will acknowledge that there will be risks associated with many activities, but risk taking is needed in order for changes to happen. Since the research and educational environment depends on the notion of change, an element of risk taking will be inherent in many activities. There will be a need to be able to assess risks and also to manage risks, if an adverse event occurs.

Risk assessment

When assessing the risk of use of a third party Web 2.0 service it is important first to clarify the purpose of the service. If the aim is to gain expertise in use of the service, then using an alternative service clearly defeats the point of the exercise. In an educational context we may find that use of a service is intended to provide exposure to it, perhaps in order to understand its limitations. The service might also provide benefits that can only be realised if it is used by large numbers of users. Social bookmarking services, such as Delicious, and social sharing services, such as Flickr and YouTube, benefit from the large numbers of users who help to rank their favourite resources and provide access to them by community agreement on common tags. In these cases, hosting such services internally will fail to deliver key benefits which the externally hosted services provide.

There is also a need to avoid making use of guidelines that have been shown to be inapplicable in a Web 2.0 context. A good example of this is the Web Content Accessibility Guidelines (WCAG), which were developed by the Web Accessibility Initiative (WAI) to help provide widely accessible web resources. A conservative approach would treat these guidelines as mandatory, and would shy away from services in which, for example, users could create content that did not comply with the WCAG guidelines or services that made use of JavaScript to provide more usable interfaces. However, Michael Cooper (WAI) admitted to the limitations of the WCAG guidelines (released in 1998) in a Web 2.0 environment in a paper on the accessibility of emerging rich web technologies presented at the W4A 2007 conference:

> However, we recognize that standards are slow, and technology evolves quickly in the commercial marketplace. Innovation brings new customers and solidifies relationships with existing customers; Web 2.0 innovations also bring new types of professionals to the field, ones who care about the new dynamic medium. As technologies prove themselves, standardizing brings in the universality of the benefit, but necessarily follows this innovation. Therefore, this paper acknowledges and respects Web 2.0, discussing the issues and real world solutions.
>
> Cooper, 2007

Related to risks regarding the accessibility of services are the legal risks associated with use of a third party service. There are risks in allowing third parties who are not affiliated to your organisation to create content on your services, such as commenting on blog posts, adding content to wikis, uploading images and so on. The risks might involve the uploading of copyrighted materials, illegal materials and materials containing personal information either to your services or to third party services associated with your organisation, which may then face the potential danger of being sued by copyright holders or aggrieved individuals, or seeing damage to your organisation's brand and identity.

Once again it would be very easy to become despondent over the legal risks associated with use of Web 2.0 technologies, which make it much easier for individuals to create content or reuse others' content. Yet in reality, might the concerns turn out to be over-stated? Are there ways in which such risks can be managed? When the web became popular in the mid-1990s there were concerns that caches, which held copies of resources in order to enhance the performance of slow networks, would breach copyright. Similarly, in 1996 a dispute between the *Shetland News* and the *Shetland Times* about deep-linking to web pages caused concerns that links to web pages should not be made without first seeking written permission. But we now find ourselves in an environment in which caches are an integral part of the web's infrastructure and web authors routinely link to pages without being concerned about possible copyright infringement – or, in those cases in which there is an understanding of reasons why organisations may have concerns regarding deep-linking, the approach taken is likely to be a willingness to remove the links if the copyright holder makes such a request.

Finally, it should be understood that there may be risks in doing nothing or in continuing to use current technologies. This might include losing one's competitive edge, lost opportunity costs and a loss of one's user communities to services that are willing to take risks.

Risk management

A risk assessment exercise can help to clarify the risks associated with the selection of Web 2.0 services. This risk assessment needs to be complemented with a risk management strategy, which will document the processes to be adopted if the risks that have been identified actually occur.

There are several approaches that can be taken to the risk management of Web 2.0 services including:

- *Use in experimental areas*: Web 2.0 services can be used in experimental areas, in which an element of risk is deemed acceptable. Such experimentation might include the evaluation of new services.

- *Engagement with users in the risks*: A useful strategy might be to engage your user in the risk-taking. Users may be willing to take part in the evaluation of new services and to provide their views on the service.

- *Data migration*: The normal approach to risk management is to ensure that data held in the service can be easily migrated to alternative services.

- *Transfer to alternative solutions*: Not all services will necessarily create data that needs to be migrated. There may be services that can be replaced by alternatives if the original service is not sustainable.

- *Willingness to forego service*: Users may decide that although they make use of a service, if it disappeared they would not feel the need for it to be replaced by an equivalent alternative.

- *Willingness to discard data*: Users may be willing to accept the loss of their data. Note that this may be the case when individuals leave an institution and no longer have access to services hosted by it.

If the intention is to migrate data to new services, it is desirable to test the data migration in a controlled, managed fashion, rather than leaving this to a time when a service has announced that it is to close in a short period of time. Such testing should identify possible limitations in the data migration. In the case of a blogging service, for example, you may find that although blog posts can be migrated easily, associated comments are lost together with details of the author of the post. Such experimentation may help to identify various strategies for the data migration, ranging from the import or export of RSS feeds through to the transfer of the HTML representation of the service.

Case studies

Case study 1 'Amplification' of the Institutional Web Management Workshop 2009 event

Organisations that are willing to exploit the potential offered by externally hosted Web 2.0 services, but which recognise that this may entail some risks, would be advised to document their analysis of potential risks and to describe their plans if such risks occur.

An example of this approach was taken by the organisers of UKOLN's Institutional Web Management Workshop (IWMW), an annual event aimed at members of institutional web management teams in UK universities. The IWMW 2009 event, held at the University of Essex in July 2009, provided the organisers with an opportunity to exploit the availability of a wi-fi network at this three-day event and to evaluate the potential of a variety of Web 2.0 technologies with 200 delegates whose area of professional interest is in the managing institutional web services. This 'amplified event' (Wikipedia, 2009) made use of a wi-fi network to allow discussions about the talks and sharing of the accompanying resources to be 'amplified' for the delegates at the event and to a remote audience watching the accompanying live video streaming of the plenary talks and engaging in discussions on the Twitter event backchannel.

Since this user community would have an interest in learning more about innovative web technologies, it was felt that the event would provide an opportunity to explore the potential of a variety of services. The approach taken towards potential risk was to document the reasons for the provision of the services, the potential risks and ways in which the risks could be addressed. This information, which is also published on the IWMW 2009 website (*http://iwmw.ukoln.ac.uk/iwmw 2009/risk-assessment/*), is summarised below.

Reasons for deploying Web 2.0 services

UKOLN provides a variety of externally hosted services on its IWMW 2009 website for a number of reasons, including: supporting UKOLN's role in evaluating new technologies and advising its user communities; providing richer experiences to the user community by making use of services that would be difficult or expensive to provide locally; to gain experiences of the services in order to help decide whether such services should be deployed to support future activities; and to engage with its user communities in discussing the potential benefits and risks of the tools.

User benefits

Delegates at the event would have the opportunity to gain exposure to a number of new services and would be able to evaluate the services for use within their own institution. The services would also enhance the quality of the event in a variety of ways, including improving the communications channels at the event and providing better mechanisms for sharing resources, such as reports about the event and photographs.

Risk management for 'amplified events'

In addition to documenting potential risks of use of various Web 2.0 services, such as SlideShare, consideration was also given to possible user concerns. Delegates at the event who did not want to be photographed or appear on the streaming video were invited to sit in a 'quiet zone'. As well as providing an area that respected privacy, in this area of the lecture theatre delegates were requested to avoid making use of laptop PCs, which may be distracting to others.

Case study 2 Archiving pebble blogs

A case study on archiving pebble blogs (Trafford, 2007) provides an interesting example of the problems of sustainability of a blogging service based on open source software installed locally. In this case open source blogging software had been installed locally to support a project activity. However, after the project had finished the resource costs of supporting the blogging software were found to be too great, especially as there was no funding stream to cover the work. It was therefore decided to migrate the data to a static website before removing the blog application. The case study document describes the steps that were taken in order to migrate the content to a static website. Of particular interests are the summaries of the lessons learnt from this work:

- Small-scale innovations can help to identify the potential for new services and provide motivation for larger-scale deployment.

- However, there may be resource implications if an experimental service proves popular.

- There may be a need to migrate an experimental service to a more reliable service for use in a service capacity.

- It can be useful to identify migration strategies before deploying an experimental service.

Case study 3 UK Web Focus blog

The UK Web Focus blog (*http://ukwebfocus.wordpress.com/*) provides a forum for thoughts and discussions primarily on matters relating to Web 2.0. The blog is hosted on the Wordpress.com service.

Risks of inappropriate content

There are risks in allowing unmoderated comments to be made on the blog. Most automated spam messages are trapped by the Akismet spam filter. However, occasional spam messages do get through and are displayed on the blog, and may contain links to inappropriate materials. Such comments are normally spotted and removed shortly after they appear, but there is a risk that spam could remain on the blog for a longer period, for example when the owner is away on holiday. However, it has been decided that such risks are low and the intended target audience for the blog will not be unduly shocked by such messages and would be able to appreciate that this content is not the responsibility of the blog owner.

Risks of loss of long term access to the service

A more important issue may be the sustainability of the contents of the blog, which is reliant on the WordPress.com service. In order to ensure that a feasible data migration strategy is available so the contents of the blog are not lost if the WordPress.com service becomes unavailable or changes its terms and conditions, a number of options have been explored.

Initially a back-up copy of the blog posts was set up on the Vox.com blog service. The posts were copied periodically from the WordPress.com blog to Vox.com. On further investigation of the new service it was found that the blog posts appeared to have migrated satisfactorily. However, accompanying comments were not copied. In addition, images stored on the WordPress.com service had not been copied and links in the new blog pointed back to images and other resources held on the WordPress.com service.

Another approach taken to creating a back-up of the blog was to use an offline browser program. The WinTrack software was used to copy all resources on the UK Web Focus WordPress.com website. This appeared to work correctly, copying not only the blog posts but also comments and images. However, the end result was a static HTML resource, and not a copy of the blogging environment.

The final approach was to use WordPress's export functionality to create an XML dump containing a representation of the content of the blog. This file was then imported into a local installation of the WordPress software.

Risks of dependencies on the author

Although the UK Web Focus blog is a funded activity, which supports the aims of UKOLN, the author's host institution, the content of the blog is not subject to editorial and checking processes. The blog also has a personal, conversational tone, which reflects the views of the author; these are not necessarily endorsed across the host organisation.

How are the risks that the author may publish inappropriate content without the checks and balances that an editor of a traditional newsletter would provide to be addressed? And what would happen to the content if the author left the institution to move to another one or fell out with the institution?

These risks have been addressed in the blog's policy statement (UK Web Focus, 2007). The risks of the author publishing inappropriate content are analogous to the author giving similar views in a talk. The author's professional integrity and reputation will help to ensure that a professional approach to the blog is maintained. The blog's policy also makes it clear that the content is owned jointly by the author and the host institution – if the author leaves, the documented policy makes it clear that a copy of the blog will be provided for the institution.

A risk assessment toolkit

These case studies illustrate a variety of approaches that have been taken to assessing the risks associated with the use of Web 2.0 services and documenting strategies for managing such risks.

A toolkit has been developed for organisations that wish to exploit the benefits of Web 2.0 services, while taking a managed approach to risk, based on these experiences:

- *Purpose*: Documenting the purposes of the service can help to clarify why you need to make use of Web 2.0 solutions rather than using existing solutions.

- *User awareness of risks*: You may have a responsibility to ensure that your users are made aware of potential risks in using the service. This will be particularly relevant if users create data that can potentially be lost.

- *User acceptance of risks*: It can be useful to engage your users actively in discussing the risks.

- *User education*: You should ensure that you provide your users with any training they require in best practice and effective use of the services you are providing.

- *Provision of alternatives*: You may provide multiple alternatives to services that may be at risk.

- *Willingness to discard data or services*: You may decide that you are prepared to accept loss of data or a service.

- *Data migration*: If services are likely to give notice of changes to their terms and conditions you may decide to migrate the data if this happens.

- *Risks of doing nothing*: You may decide that the risks of doing nothing and the associated missed opportunity costs are greater than the risks of using a Web 2.0 service.

An example of how this toolkit could be used for the case of the IWMW 2009 and related event is shown in Figure 5.1.

A risks and opportunities framework

We have outlined risk assessment and risk management approaches to exploiting the potential of Web 2.0 services. A risks and opportunities framework has been developed at UKOLN, which provides a structure for supporting the accompanying discussions and decision-making processes (Kelly, 2009a).

The framework is based on the notion that it will not be possible to innovate without a willingness to be prepared to

Figure 5.1 Use of risk acceptance toolkit for IWMW 2009 event

- *Purpose*: A variety of Web 2.0 services has been provided to support IWMW 2009 in order to enrich the event by providing services (such as chat facilities) that would not otherwise be available.

- *User awareness*: A web page providing details of the various services was provided before the event and participants were notified in advance.

- *User acceptance*: Participants were made aware of the potential risks and an acceptable use policy was provided.

- *User education*: Participants had the opportunity to make use of a number of the tools in advance of the event. In addition a training session was provided before it started.

- *Provision of alternatives*: Google Analytics and Site Meter services provide usage statistics for the websites (in addition to conventional web server log files).

- *Willingness to discard data*: Certain data, such as chat services and informal discussions on the wiki, was felt to be of limited interest in the longer term, and so no steps were taken to preserve it.

- *Data migration*: The access control for information on the wiki created by the discussion groups was tightened up after the event and the data was copied to a managed environment.

- *Risk of doing nothing*: It was felt that there was a danger of UKOLN losing credibility if it was not seen to be playing a leading role in evaluating innovative Web 2.0 technologies and being able to advise its communities on best practices.

take risks – after all avoiding risks may also result in missed opportunities. Rather than seeking to avoid risks completely the challenge is to understand and evaluate the risks. Once the risks have been assessed, approaches for managing these risks can be identified.

The key components of the risks and opportunities framework are illustrated in Figure 5.2.

The key components are the identification of:

- the *purpose* of the service
- the *benefits* to the various stakeholders
- the *risks* to the various stakeholders

Figure 5.2 Risks and opportunities framework for the social web

Source: Kelly, 2009b

- the *missed opportunities* in failing to take the risks

- the *costs* and associated resource implications

- approaches taken to *minimising risks* that have been identified

- gathering of *evidence* related to the components in the framework.

It should be acknowledged that in making use of the risks and opportunities framework, subjective factors including prejudices and biases will be expressed.

Using the framework

Two examples illustrate use of this framework.

Use of Twitter by an individual

- *Purpose*: Individual use of Twitter by staff in an organisation in order to support community building with peers across the sector.

- *Benefits*: Being part of an active community of practice can help an individual's professional development. The ability to share successes can help to promote an organisation, and having a pool of experts can be beneficial when seeking help and advice.

- *Risks*: There may be dangers that excessive amounts of time are spent using Twitter. It may also be used for non-work-related purposes.

- *Missed opportunities*: A failure to permit motivated individuals to use Twitter to support their professional activities may demotivate them and result in a failure to exploit the benefits of a community of practice.

- *Costs*: There should be no licensing costs for software. The costs are primarily staff time.

Use of Facebook by an organisation

- *Purpose*: Organisational use of Facebook in order to promote the organisation.

- *Benefits*: Facebook users can become fans of an organisation's page, thus establishing a relationship with that organisation's community. Information on news, events and so on can be provided without the need to set up and maintain a web presence. The Facebook wall allows users to send messages and establish a dialogue with the organisation.

- *Risks*: The Facebook terms and conditions allow Facebook to exploit commercially content that has been uploaded. This may infringe the rights of copyright holders if, for example, images are uploaded to Facebook. It may be difficult to migrate content uploaded to Facebook to other environments. Maintenance of content and responding to messages may be time-consuming. In addition, maintenance will require access to Facebook, which may be blocked in some organisations. Some users may regard Facebook as an environment for personal use and not wish to make links to an organisational presence.

- *Missed opportunities*: A failure to provide an organisational presence on Facebook can result in missed marketing opportunities.

- *Costs*: There should be no licensing costs for software. The costs are primarily staff time.

References

Bradley, P. (2010) 100 British librarians on Twitter, *http://tweepml .org/100-British-Librarians-on-Twitter/* (accessed 7 January 2010).

Cooper, M. (2007) *Accessibility of Emerging Rich Web Technologies: Web 2.0 and the semantic web,* World Wide Web Consortium Web Accessibility Initiative, *http://www.w4a.info/ 2007/prog/k3-cooper.pdf* (accessed 7 January 2010).

Evans, J. (2009) Guest post: blogs at Imperial College, UK Web Focus blog, 2 October, *http://ukwebfocus.wordpress.com/2009/ 10/02/guest-post-blogs-at-imperial-college/* (accessed 5 February 2010).

Kelly, B. (2007) When two tribes go to war, UK Web Focus blog, 22 November, *http://ukwebfocus.wordpress.com/2007/11/22/ when-two-tribes-go-to-war/* (accessed 8 January 2010).

Kelly, B. (2009a) Time to stop doing and start thinking: a framework for exploiting Web 2.0 service, *http://www.ukoln.ac.uk/ web-focus/papers/mw-2009/* (accessed 8 January 2010).

Kelly, B. (2009b) Further developments of a risks and opportunities framework, UK Web Focus blog, 16 April, *http://ukwebfocus .wordpress.com/2009/04/16/further-developments-of-a-risks- and-opportunities-framework/* (accessed 5 February 2010).

O'Reilly, T. (2005) *What is Web 2.0?: design patterns and business models for the next generation of software,* 30 September, *http://www.oreilly.com/pub/a/oreilly/tim/news/2005/09/30/ what-is-web-20.html* (accessed 8 January 2010).

Trafford, P. (2007) *Archiving Pebble Blogs at Ramble.oucs,* QA Focus Case Study 36, UKOLN, *http://www.ukoln.ac.uk/qa-focus/ documents/case-studies/case-study-36/* (accessed 8 January 2010).

UK Web Focus (2007) Policies for this blog, *http://ukwebfocus .wordpress.com/policies/* (accessed 8 January 2010).

Wikipedia (2009) Amplified conference, *http://en.wikipedia.org/ wiki/Amplified_conference* (accessed 8 January 2010).

6

Emerging technologies for learning

David Ley

It is not the person ignorant of writing but the one ignorant of photography who will be the illiterate of the future.

Laszlo Moholy-Nagy

Introduction

This chapter investigates the issue surrounding the increasing use of new digital technologies, for example social networking, in the lives of learners outside the formal education setting and argues that it is becoming a natural and useful experience. It is argued that technology in itself is not good or bad, but may have good and bad effects, many of which will be unintended and unforeseen.

The debate on IT is also explored, including its development from mainframe to handheld devices, and its impact. This debate is not new and echoes ancient arguments made by the likes of Socrates, who bemoaned the invention of the alphabet, believing it would affect students' ability to engage in meaningful dialogue. Many new and potential technologies are examined, in particular the potential of the semantic web (Web 3.0) and the mobile web.

The debate about technology and its utility is discussed and considered to be over; now there is a focus on how best to use the potential of new technologies to have a positive impact on education. What is needed are agile systems, which balance what education needs and what technology can do in an informed synergy where learners control their own learning; technology is most exciting and most transformational when it enables us to do something previously impossible. These novel possibilities include new types of community and collaboration, dialogue, co-construction of knowledge, and new styles of creativity. The chapter moves on to explore how the widespread adoption of digital technologies has had an impact on learners, businesses and people in general. However, it is not all plain sailing and the barriers and problems in implementing new technologies are examined.

The discourse below also highlights the ways in which new technologies, especially the potential of social networking, match many parts of the educational agenda and indeed pedagogical theories such as Vygotsky's social constructivism and Seymour Papert's constructionism. How these approaches can be implemented, particularly constructivist approaches, can be seen in Chapter 3. It is argued that these developments plus the increasingly visual nature of interfaces can influence and shape learning, learner autonomy, motivation and engagement. Although it investigates and explores the plethora of new developments, this chapter also explores the issue of the changing nature of young learners and argues that 'digital natives', the 'net generation' and the new knowledge workers have a new way of learning and that increasingly they seek problems to solve rather than knowledge to apply. In all, this chapter provides an informed journey into the landscape of new technologies and the users who inhabit it.

The invention of photography changed our understanding of the world and our perception of it. Photographs did not actually capture reality, but gave us a new view of another 'virtual' world. So the technology changed the way we relate to the world and each other. It allowed Muybridge to investigate the gait of a galloping horse and by putting the means to make pictures in everybody's hands, let us all capture the 'decisive moment'.

Today, digital information and communication technologies are having a similar and even more profound effect, allowing the 'annihilation of space and time' (Alexander Pope). They are visibly and invisibly a part of all aspects of modern life and their effects resonate across the boundaries that used to separate work from home, learning from pleasure. Most technology is not conceived or designed for education; it has a life of its own and impacts on society and culture over time. Learners are increasingly using new digital technologies in their lives outside formal education and these are becoming a natural and useful part of their experience. Education can no longer control or limit technology use to a defined set of tools, or it risks becoming irrelevant to 21st-century learners.

A classic essay question is 'Does technology control society or does society control technology?'. Of course this is a false dichotomy, as both are inextricably intertwined and influence and inform each other in a synergistic relationship. However, society and therefore education changes more slowly than technology. Technology itself is not good or bad, but will have good and bad effects, many of them unintended.

Despite this, we need to guard against technology determinism. The problems of education cannot be easily fixed by simply applying technology. In recent years many have talked about the speed of technological change, even exponential change. However, other than for the increase in the number of transistors on a chip (Moore's Law), this rarely holds true. Often our perspective is skewed and we overestimate the impact of the new and underestimate the impact of older technologies (Seidensticker, 2006).

Conversely, by denying change and not accepting the potential of new technologies and approaches, technology detractors risk making education irrelevant to learners, the needs of society and the increasingly globalised economy. These debates about new technologies are not new: Socrates bemoaned the invention of the alphabet, which he thought would prevent his students from memorising information and reduce the quality of their dialogue (Socrates, 470 BC).

The argument about whether digital technologies should be used in education should now be over. The debate is moving to how best to use the clear potential of technologies to have a positive impact on education, so a balance is needed between what education needs and what technology can do. Both need to inform each other, so that we can create an agile system that understands the power of technology, understands its learners and learning, and creates future citizens with the power to control their own learning. In Chapter 4 Jenny Yorke and Helen Walmsley explore how staff effort can be maximised, and in Chapter 3 Geoff Walton looks at the emerging e-pedagogy to support deliver online learning opportunities.

> The illiterate of the future will not be the person who cannot read. It will be the person who does not know how to learn.
>
> Alvin Toffler

Technology in education has often been used to digitise existing practice, and it is most exciting and transformational when it enables us to do something that was previously impossible. This chapter looks at three new types of technology-mediated interaction and learning: new kinds of community and collaboration, dialogue and co-construction of knowledge, and new styles of creativity. It goes on to explore the impact that the widespread adoption of digital technologies has had on learners, businesses and people in general.

Web 2.0 and social software

The term Web 2.0 (attributed to Dale Dougherty, of O'Reilly Media, but extended and popularised by Tim O'Reilly of the same company), although loosely defined, describes a range of technologies, services, trends and behaviours that have evolved to create what is sometimes called the read/write web. Becta has described Web 2.0:

> It is about using the internet as a platform for simple, light-weight services that leverage social interactions for communication, collaboration, and creating, remixing and sharing content. Typically, these services develop rapidly, often relying on a large community of users to create and add value to content or data. The availability and ease of use of Web 2.0 tools and services has lowered the barriers to production and distribution of content. Some examples of Web 2.0 services include: social networking sites, blogs, wikis, social bookmarking, media sharing sites, rich internet applications and web 'mashups'.

> Becta, 2008

This shift in the web from being about passive consumption of information to more active participation is claimed by

Tim Berners Lee always to have been part of the vision for the web. But this more participatory web has only become possible because of the critical mass of broadband-connected users (supported by inexpensive PCs, cheap storage, internet innovators and media convergence). Indeed, most of the technology behind Web 2.0 is not new, but is being used in new ways to enable new social interactions.

Paul Anderson has taken the range of Web 2.0 type approaches – blogs, wikis, social networking, podcasting, social bookmarking, content creation and sharing, user-defined tagging, rich internet applications and open access to data and programming interfaces – and identified six key ideas or characteristics that define them (Anderson, 2007):

- individual production and user-generated content
- harnessing the power of the crowd
- data on an epic scale
- architecture of participation
- network effects
- openness.

We know that many learners are using Web 2.0 websites and services in their lives outside formal education (Lenhart and Madden, 2005; Dutton and Helsper, 2007; Ofcom, 2007). However, the question has been whether these approaches can be used in education to improve the learning experience and, if so, what the barriers and issues are in their implementation.

Web 2.0 has received a great deal of attention from educationalists, as its attributes seem to match many parts of the educational agenda and indeed pedagogical theories such as Vygotsky's social constructivism (Vygotsky, 1978) and Seymour Papert's constructionism (Papert, 1980). More research is needed into the impact of learning of using Web 2.0 tools and services. For example, does this collaborative model of learning suit all learners? It has been estimated that only around 1 per cent of the users of most sites regularly make contributions (BBC News, 2007). Are the communities created usually made up of the same type of people from the same background? Are they in fact reinforcing their own prejudices and subjective views?

Web 2.0 characteristics match many of the aims of the personalising learning agenda (Leadbeater, 2005; Gilbert, 2006), allowing learners to take more control of their own learning (learner autonomy), and directly access their own customised sources of information, data, tools and services.

Personalising learning is about:

> providing greater customisation, match to individual needs and greater choice and opportunity for learners and developing more responsive and flexible arrangements for learning both in and outside of the formal curriculum in schools, colleges, higher education, skills training and lifelong learning.
>
> Becta, 2007

Just as Web 2.0 applications are now being offered to business, learning management system providers are also adding the functionality to their products. Education-specific products certainly offer advantages for school age learners where the issue of control and e-safety are perhaps more paramount than for higher education. However, many proponents of Web 2.0 approaches for education argue that the current organisation of learning around instructor-led units does not necessarily fit well with the more organic, collaborative, bottom-up style of Web 2.0. Lee Bryant believes Web 2.0 development will go together with a change in educational focus: 'the peak of... e-learning "content delivery" systems will coincide with the peak of target-driven, test-based education policy, and what follows will be more personal and aimed towards a broader set of personal development goals in both technology and pedagogy' (Bryant, 2007).

One response to this has been the idea of the personal learning environment, which builds on the Web 2.0 idea of 'small pieces loosely joined' (Weinberger, 2002a; CETIS, 2005). The personal learning environment is a loose collection of tools, services, people and resources, which harness the power of the network.

Increasingly it is felt that 21st-century learning needs to evolve to create learners suited to the new priorities of the world of work, who are digitally literate and able to adapt and learn throughout their lives. Web 2.0, with its ability to help foster the building of communities of learning, encourage collaboration, co-creation and sharing, and to make it easy to connect to networks of people, information and services, seems to fit well with this model:

> All learning technology will be at least to some degree network technology, since it is designed to facilitate the interaction between public knowledge and personal knowledge... learning technology that promotes autonomy, encourages diversity, enables interaction and supports openness will, in the main, be more effective than technology that does not.
>
> Downes, 2007

The use of Web 2.0 in education is only just beginning to be explored through small-scale trials by innovative practitioners and some more institutional-level implementations and evidence of impact is limited (Crook and Harrison, 2008). The potential of these approaches is clear, but there remains a range of issues to be addressed. There are technical and security issues around the use of consumer services that do not have service level agreements, robust security or back-ups, but it is not yet clear whether education-specific Web 2.0 approaches that could offer this level of control negate the advantages of learner autonomy in being able to select and integrate their own set of tools. Intellectual property rights, copyright issues and concerns over control of hosting, content and interoperability worry IT managers. For teachers there are issues to do with how collaborative work is preserved and assessed, and what pedagogies are most appropriate to Web 2.0 integration. There are very real concerns over e-safety, cyber-bullying, child protection and privacy.

It has been suggested that learners today may have a different notion of privacy from older users. An article in *New York Magazine* (Nussbaum, 2007) discusses how American youth were more relaxed about their details being available on the net. Indeed they accepted that they had an audience online. However, learners need to be made aware of the potential consequences of what they publish online. For example, the notion of 'digital persistency' – that information published online lasts forever and cannot be readily deleted – is not always appreciated by students. At Warwick University, where all students are given a blog space, student bloggers may not be so keen on potential employers being able to read about their weekend exploits after a quick Google search. Students may now be putting great efforts into maintaining their online reputations, but their audience at the time of writing may be different from that in the future.

Web 3.0?

Although the term Web 2.0 suggests a future technology, it is no longer an emerging technology. It is simply the web today. Discussion has already moved to Web 3.0. This has no clear definition as yet, but is commonly accepted to be about the semantic web and/or the 3D web. The semantic web is about giving meaning to web data so that it can be retrieved and understood by machines or applications that can then draw connections between disparate pieces of information. This would be an important part of enabling the intelligent agents (proactive, autonomous, software tools and systems that can determine appropriate actions based on a range of data from multiple sources) that would work for us in the full vision of ubiquitous computing (see 'Ubiquitous computing', below). However, many believe the requirements of the semantic web are too onerous, too rigid and unachievable (Weinberger, 2002b; Shirky, 2003).

The beginnings of a more visual, 3D web can be seen in online virtual worlds such as Second Life. Many companies such as IBM and Cisco are exploring the possibilities of this new way of presenting information and interacting online, and universities and schools are also beginning to experiment with innovative approaches in these 'metaverses' (Twining, 2007).

Social software on mobile devices

As the internet has extended to our mobile devices, so too has social software. Mobile Web 2.0 applications are now seen as a major driver for the uptake of the mobile internet. Mobile devices now offer a pervasive and trusted interface, the social aspects of which have already made them a natural and personal extension of our lives. The mobile web means people today are connected to a permanent 'info-cloud' (Wal, 2009) of information, services and people, which has interesting socio-cultural implications. Using friend locator services, mobile blogging and micro-blogging sites like Twitter, people are seeing the world, their actions and relationships through a new lens of declarative living (Squidoo, n.d.).

Mobile learning

Mobile devices are now a widely accepted and invaluable part of modern life and there has been interest in using them to enable flexible, anytime, anywhere learning for some time. However, now a variety of devices are likely to be in the pockets of learners, the potential for employing mobile learning has greatly increased. Mobile learning is about much more than just delivering digital learning content to a mobile device. It enables new ways of learning and digitally enhanced experiences across different contexts. Education needs to explore ways of using the power of these increasingly available devices, while addressing some of the issues such as equality of access and management overheads.

The range and functionality of mobile devices continues to improve. They include laptops, netbooks and tablet PCs, but it is handheld devices that could offer the greatest opportunities for learning in new ways. The proliferation of these devices beyond the personal digital assistants means that learning devices today could include mobile phones, smartphones, ultra-mobile PCs and mobile internet devices, handheld games consoles, internet tablets, media players, e-book readers and digital cameras.

The boundaries between learning, working, socialising and entertainment, and where and when these activities take place, are increasingly blurred. Similarly, the roles and functionality of mobile devices have converged, as they are all likely to have to meet diverse needs of users. Having said that, devices still broadly fit into three categories, albeit with overlapping capabilities:

- computer-centric devices, such as personal digital assistants and ultra-mobile PCs

- communication-centric devices such as mobile phones and smart phones

- entertainment-centric devices such as games consoles, media players and e-book readers.

In general, devices are becoming more powerful, more connected and more versatile. Typically all these devices can now offer a range of functionality, such as wireless connectivity, more powerful processors and applications, multimedia capabilities, integrated cameras, content creation tools, GPS and sensors.

At the same time some of the barriers of mobile devices – poor battery life, small displays, difficult interfaces and high cost – are beginning to be addressed.

Battery life

Battery life is improving through the use of more efficient components and designs. Energy efficiency is now a key driver for processor and chipset manufacturers and simpler system on a chip (SoC) designs will decrease size and power requirements. The move towards solid state hard drives and emerging display technologies (see below) also help. New battery designs, super capacitors and micro fuel cells have yet to reach market, but hold some promise for the future.

Displays

The size, resolution and brightness of mobile displays has gradually improved, but have always been limited by the size of the device itself. Developments in organic LED (OLED) and light-emitting polymer displays offer great potential in this area. These displays, already used in a small number of devices, are electroluminescent, so don't require a backlight, and are extremely thin and bright. By putting these displays on flexible substrates, manufacturers have shown prototypes of rollable displays. This offers the promise of displays that can be larger than the mobile device itself.

Electronic paper

Electronic paper, which offers high resolution paper like reflective displays, is being used in a new range of e-book readers. Currently, slow and monochrome, developers are considering adding colour and transition speeds fast enough for use as general displays. Again, flexible versions of electronic paper could offer large, inexpensive displays, which could be formed to fit in a variety of innovative applications. Other display technologies for mobile devices currently emerging are heads-up displays and integrated nano projectors.

Interfaces

On the desktop the interface has remained focused on the keyboard and mouse. There have been developments in handwriting recognition, voice recognition, gesture recognition, haptics, eye-tracking and wearable computers. These have not become mainstream because of usability issues and the fact that in most situations and for most users they do not offer a compelling advantage or improvement in productivity. However, for smaller mobile devices the desktop model is inappropriate (despite the persistence of miniature keyboards).

Developments are happening in two main areas. The first is the physical interface, where some of the technologies mentioned above are beginning to appear. For example, an increasing number of mobile devices now have touch screens. The next step will be to use haptics technologies to add 'feel' to the touch screen displays. Accelerometers that detect movement (as seen in the Wii controller) are also being deployed in mobiles (research from InStat suggests that MEMS (micro-electro-mechanical systems) in mobile handsets will be worth $1 billion by 2010 (In Stat, 2006). The second main area of development is that of rethinking the visual interface itself, to minimise the need for text input and to have smarter systems that understand what the user is trying to achieve. Eventually miniature cameras coupled with human scale storage opens the possibility of life-recorders, for example Microsoft Sensecam (*http://research.microsoft .com/en-us/um/cambridge/projects/ sensecam/*).

Cost

As with most technologies the price of mobile devices has fallen and performance has improved. However, more recently there has been an effort to produce low-cost devices aimed at education, particularly in the developing world. The One Laptop per Child (OLPC; *http://www.laptop.org/*) scheme to create a rugged $100 laptop for the developing world is now taking orders (if at nearer $150 per laptop). Other companies are also offering low-cost devices such as the new range of inexpensive, small notebook computers known as netbooks.

Connectivity

Wireless connectivity transforms mobile devices and enables anytime, anywhere networked learning and learner interactions. Many future visions of education are predicated on there being ubiquitous access to inexpensive (or free), fast, reliable wireless connections. Most educational institutions now have wireless local area networks (WLANs), using wi-fi access points. In the UK, 80 per cent of secondary and 50 per cent of primary schools have wireless networks (Becta, 2007). Many people are using the same technology to share their broadband connections at home. However, outside these locations connectivity can be slow, unreliable, expensive or just unavailable. A number of technology and market developments are beginning to address some of these issues.

WiMAX

WiMAX (Worldwide Interoperability for Microwave Access) is an emerging wireless broadband technology based on IEEE 802.16 standards. There are currently two main versions: fixed or nomadic and mobile, which are incompatible with each other. Despite early hype around the technology talking of data rates of 75 Mbps over ranges of 45 km, the reality is that typical speeds will be between 1 Mbps and 10 Mbps (synchronous), delivered in WiMAX cells of 1–5 km. The mobile version has most potential and suitable licensed spectrum is being made available in many countries. Commercial WiMAX networks have now been deployed in a number of countries. Early indications are that WiMAX is likely to be priced at similar levels to fixed broadband. An upgrade to the standard (802.16 m) is expected to offer peak speeds up to 1 Gbps. In developed countries WiMAX is likely mainly to be available in urban areas and will face strong competition from mobile phone operator networks. However, in developing countries where there is no existing wired infrastructure it is seen as a technology for linking rural areas. India, for example, is planning a major deployment of WiMAX to villages that will also connect 40,000 schools.

3.5G and 3.9G

Third generation (3G) mobile phone network upgrades to GSM (global system for mobiles) were to a certain extent disappointing. Maximum data rates of 384 Kbps, limited coverage, limited 'walled garden' internet access and expensive per MB price plans largely relegated it to business users. However, an upgrade to 3G networks known as high speed packet access, or 3.5G, has improved download rates significantly. HSPA+ should increase these speeds to over 20 Mbps. Operators have also begun offering flat rate data plans and providing open internet access. The next major shift will be the move to long term evolution (LTE), also known as 3.9G. Early testing of this technology has shown speeds of 100 Mbps at very low latencies. However, this is unlikely to begin to appear until 2010–12.

Wi-fi

Wi-fi connectivity is now provided by most institutions and is found in public and commercial locations such as libraries, transport systems, cafés, bars, restaurants, hotels and airports. Some cities have implemented municipal wireless schemes to provide coverage over a large area for public sector workers, infrastructure management and citizen access. Standards keep developing with the faster 802.11n having been ratified in September 2009. However, the standards process is widely seen as too slow and cumbersome and many manufacturers are moving towards testing interoperability themselves and releasing products before full ratification of final standards.

4G

Fourth generation networks have not yet been fully defined by the International Telecommunication Union, but it is expected to specify 100 Mbps mobile connectivity. What is more certain is that 4G will be an all IP-based technology, also using orthogonal frequency-division multiple access (OFDMA) and multiple-input, multiple-output (MIMO) communications. Both WiMAX and Long Term Evolution (LTE) are strong contenders to be adopted as 4G technologies. However, the distinction between computer network technologies and mobile phone technologies will blur in 4G. Already the two camps are starting to adopt each other's technologies. It is likely that 4G devices will actually be able to roam seamlessly between a variety of different network technologies, selecting the most appropriate connection at any one time, depending on availability, application and cost.

Personal area networks

Short range, ad-hoc wireless connections between mobile devices, computers and peripherals have been dominated by relatively slow Bluetooth connections. Developments are addressing three main areas: speed, power requirements and security and ease of use. Although ultra wideband (UWB), a low-power, short range (<10 m), high speed, cable replacement technology, has failed to take off, a number of other wireless technologies with similar characteristics have been developed. Near Field Communication (NFC) is also likely to appear in increasing numbers of mobile devices for mobile commerce applications such as ticketing and e-payments.

The mobile internet

Until very recently, the mobile internet had struggled to become a reality for the majority of users, because of the high costs, poor interfaces on mobile devices and limits imposed by operators. However, there is an increasing trend towards devices that can deliver the full internet experience, supported by operators offering flat rate data tariffs, with fewer restrictions on access. In a speech at the Mobile Internet World conference in 2007, Tim Berners-Lee called for vendors to adopt open standards for the mobile internet and avoid proprietary technologies (Hamblen, 2007).

Competition for control of the mobile internet between hardware manufacturers, network operators (who fear becoming merely 'bit pipes'), software vendors and internet companies is intense. This can only help drive innovation and lower prices for users. Location-based services, social software, mobile commerce and unified communications are expected to continue to increase use.

Impact on learning

Many projects have looked at how to use these new mobile and personal technologies to improve learning (Naismith et al., 2004). These are some of the benefits of using them:

- *flexible access*: can be used where and when needed, in and outside the classroom

- *embed ICT in classrooms*: quick deployment; take up little space; easy for ad-hoc use; user centred; immediate access to information and tools (many devices offer instant-on); ad-hoc collaboration

- *learner autonomy*: 1:1 access to ICT; 'ownership' encourages student-initiated learning and sense of responsibility; can enable learner autonomy and help deliver personalised learning

- *improve home–school links*: help engage parents in learning process; potentially tackle digital divide

- *motivation, engagement*: evidence of increased motivation, particularly for boys

- *situated learning*: facilitate location- and context-based learning (e.g. field trips, museums), ambient learning, mediascapes and augmented reality (see below).

Mike Sharples has noted the fit between current educational priorities and the attributes of mobile learning (Sharples, Taylor and Vavoula, 2005):

Educational priority	Mobile learning
Personalised	Personal
Learner-centred	User-centred
Situated	Mobile
Collaborative	Networked
Ubiquitous	Ubiquitous
Life-long	Durable

However, there is still much discussion (e.g. Pachler, 2007) on what learning mediated by personal digital device means. It seems to be about more than having ubiquitous access to learning opportunities and raises questions about how far these approaches fit with the structured curriculum and assessment systems prevalent today. There is evidence of benefit, but not yet transformation.

Ubiquitous computing

> The most profound technologies are those that disappear. They weave themselves into the fabric of everyday life until they are indistinguishable from it.
>
> Weiser, 1991

Ubiquitous computing, pervasive computing, calm computing, invisible computing, ambient computing and the real world web are all terms used to describe a vision of miniature connected processors and sensors embedded in objects, devices and locations in the world around us and working for us, often without the need for explicit interaction: 'Its highest ideal is to make a computer so embedded, so fitting, so natural, that we use it even without thinking about it' (Weiser, 1991).

Weiser and Brown (1996) described three waves of computing: the mainframe wave, when many people shared a computer; the personal computer wave, when each person has their own computer; and finally the ubiquitous computing wave, where each person shares many computers, most of which remain invisible. This implies a major shift to a more human centred relationship with computers, with technology working for us, adapting to our needs and preferences, but remaining invisible until needed. This new computing power needs to be accessed through new intelligent interfaces that are adaptable, responsive and intuitive to use.

Weiser was writing before the advent of the internet and mobile devices in every pocket and his vision has been criticised for being too complex, unnecessary and having profound social, political and ethical issues. However, even if his vision of computing seamlessly connected and deeply embedded in objects, places and devices is never quite achieved, elements of the vision are beginning to appear and offer new interactions and functionality in their own right.

The increasing performance and miniaturisation of processors, sensors, memory, networking technologies and displays is allowing more objects and devices to become addressable (have a unique ID) and connected (usually wirelessly). This new 'internet of things' (ITU, 2005) will collect huge amounts of data, and allow new interactions in the real world between people and things, between people and places, and between things and things. The web moves from being purely a virtual space to one that interacts with the real world and provides us with real time information, help and services. This should enable more personalised, context-aware interactions and smarter decisions. As will be explored, this also helps with a move to more experiential learning: learning by doing, interacting, communicating and sharing.

The ubiquitous computing world is underpinned by four main elements: identification, location, sensing and connectivity.

Identification

Unique identification is key to enabling objects and locations to be recognised and become part of a wider intelligent, information-sharing network. This also allows objects and locations to be interrogated by learners or other users, or for information to be provided automatically.

RFID

Radio frequency identification (RFID) is a generic term for technologies that use radio waves to identify objects, locations or people. In recent years it has particularly been associated with RFID tags. These are miniature microchips (as small as 0.05 mm^2) attached to transponders that can be read by transceivers. Currently these are mainly being used in the retail supply chain in order to replace barcodes. There are two main types of RFID tag:

- passive tags that harvest energy from the reader device in order to transmit their data over a distance of a few centimetres

- active tags that have their own power supply and can transmit over longer distances up to 100 m, and often have data read–write capabilities.

RFID tags allow computer systems to identify, locate and track things in the real world. This is potentially a transformational technology, although technical issues, concerns about privacy and high costs will need to be addressed before they become mainstream. RFID is already in use in retail, payment systems, contactless travel cards, security/door entry and a range of other applications. Analysts believe that many of the eventual uses of RFID have not yet been thought of today.

In education RFID is beginning to be used for some practical applications such as library management systems, asset tagging and ID cards. Indeed, some schools around the world use RFID-enabled badges to monitor student attendance and track movements (*http://ubiks.net/local/blog/ jmt/archives3/005856.html* and *http://www.sankei.co.jp/ seiji/seisaku/070103/ssk070103000.htm*), information that can even be provided to parents. However, it can also be used in more innovative learning projects allowing users to interact with objects in the real world, for example with exhibits in museums (Campbell, 2005). By bringing a mobile device close to a tagged item, information about it can be displayed on learners' screens. RFID tags are also embedded in some mobile phones and used with NFC in order to make secure connections.

2D barcodes

2D barcodes are printed 'pictures' with data embedded in them. When a photo of a 2D barcode is taken with a suitably enabled cameraphone, the user is taken to a website or provided with other data. Newer versions can be invisibly embedded into photos. They are seen as a way of hyperlinking the world, allowing users quickly and easily to interact with posters, objects, vending machines, magazine articles and so on using their mobile devices. Unlike RFID, 2D barcodes rely on explicit actions of the user, so do not have the privacy issues of RFID. Widely found in Japan, they are beginning to appear elsewhere. For example the BBC placed them on signs to provide additional content to walkers involved in the Coast project (NeoMedia, 2009). In education they have been used as an easy way to provide additional resources to learners such as lists of URLs (Fujimura and Doi, 2006), but also can be used to allow interaction with real world objects.

IPv6

Currently the internet and most other networks rely on Internet Protocol version 4 (IPv4), which has a limit of 2^{32} unique addresses. Already the Internet Corporation for Assigned Names and Numbers (ICANN) and Vint Cerf have warned that we are running dangerously short of new addresses, as China, India and other countries adopt widespread use of the internet. IPv6, the next generation protocol, largely only used by researchers and government and military organisations, offers 2^{128} unique addresses. This is enough for every device, person and object to have its own unique IP address.

Location

The ability to locate objects, devices and people in the real world not only provides a valuable layer of information about the world, but is key to enabling a new set of interactions between people, locations and computer systems and the web.

Location can be established in a variety of ways and to varying levels of accuracy. The main distinction is between systems that understand relative location (e.g. an RFID tag passing a fixed wireless reader) and those that establish absolute positions (e.g. GPS satellite navigation).

Some systems can use triangulation to pinpoint the location of wi-fi-enabled device (for example Ekahau systems (*http://www.ekahau.com/*). Mobile phones can be located using the same technique, but the accuracy will likely to be measured in hundreds of metres and may be even worse in rural areas where the cell sizes are much larger.

Satellite positioning technologies that provide absolute location information to within a few metres are now widely available in dedicated units as well as appearing in PDAs, smartphones, cameras and other objects, such as school bags or badges. A European system, known as Galileo, is also in development. It promises better coverage, more accuracy and freedom from US government control.

Most wireless systems such as RFID tags are essentially proximity based, so rely on a user or device coming near to them before an event is triggered. This 'event' could be relevant learning materials downloaded to a user's device, or automatic connection to a large display, for example. Other location services are about knowing your relationship to other people or devices. MIT's iFind service (*http://ifind .mit.edu/*) allows students and staff to let other people know their location on campus. Mobile-location-based services (*http://www.mologogo.com/*) are increasingly combining presence (information about the status of a user) with location information.

A third way of obtaining location information is scene analysis. This combines a variety of techniques, including GPS, digital compasses and camera phones. GeoVector Corporation (*http://www.geovector.com/appdemos/*) offers one such system to Japanese mobile phone users. When a mobile phone is pointed at buildings or other locations, information and services related to that place are shown on the device. A variety of innovative uses from mapping, tourist information, local search, mobile commerce, entertainment guides, shopping guides and advertising are envisaged, but these could easily be extended to educational content.

Mediascapes

Various innovative educational projects have explored the use of location-based systems to deliver context-related content to learners. These allow teachers to 'tag' content such as sound files, photos, videos or text to locations in the real world, or exhibits in museums. Using mobile devices, learners then navigate through the mediascape or learning trail with relevant content automatically delivered to their device when they reach a certain point of interest. Learners can also add their own content (or 'digital graffiti') to locations to share with others and build up understanding collaboratively. The systems often record the learning journey a student has made for later reflection in the classroom. Examples of such projects include: Mobile Bristol (*http://www.mobilebristol.com/flash.html*), Mudlarking in Deptford (*http://www.futurelab.org.uk/projects/mudlarking_ in_deptford*) and Equator (*http://www.mrl.nott.ac.uk/*). These mediascapes are relatively straightforward for teachers to create, using online tools (*http://createascape.org.uk/*).

Augmented reality

Augmented reality is about superimposing digital information onto our view of the real world. Ultimately this may be achieved with heads-up displays, or using retinal scan displays, but these have so far been restricted to specialist applications. However, augmented or mixed reality can also be implemented on mobile devices with cameras. The mobile augmented reality application (MARA; *http://research.nokia .com/research/projects/mara/index.html*) being developed by Nokia is one example and a number of other augmented reality applications are now coming to market for use on smartphones, such as Layar and Wikitude.

Sensing and sensor networks

Adding sensing to ubiquitous computing networks allows the collection of a range of real time data. By adding MEMS (micro-electro-mechanical systems) actuators can respond to events and take action.

Sensors usually measure pressure, temperature, speed, air and water quality, stress, humidity or acceleration. More recently sensors have been combined with micro-controllers, memory and radios to create sensor networks. These mesh networks of sensor nodes are self-configuring and extremely robust, making them easily scaleable to cover large areas even in harsh conditions. Many sensor networks require little power and could potentially be deployed for a number of years. Future developments in this area are focusing on the creation of 'smart dust' (Arvind and Wong, 2004). These are sensor networks with nodes, potentially as small as a grain of rice, which could quickly be deployed into a range of environments to provide real-time data.

For education these remote sensing technologies are providing opportunities for experiential learning. Instead of learning about things, learners have the opportunity to use the same data, tools and techniques as professionals. This corresponds to Bruner's concept of 'learning to be' (Bruner, 1969).

By collecting and manipulating real information from sensors in the environment, learners can take readings, analyse data, model concepts and test hypotheses. The Coastal Ocean Observation Laboratory (*http://www.coolclassroom.org/home.html*) based at Rutgers University (USA) can be accessed online, enabling learners to use and manipulate real time data collected from sensors in the ocean.

Learners are also beginning to be able to control and interact with remote locations. This currently involves video conferencing or controlling scientific equipment. For example, the MIT iLab (*http://icampus.mit.edu/ilabs/*) allows students to conduct experiments remotely over the internet. The Bradford robotic telescope (*http://www.telescope.org/*) allows learners to request images from a professional space telescope located in Tenerife. An evaluation of the project found that it was:

> a new type of learning website supported by a real world facility which provides real time access to operational data to support learning programmes. The learner has a degree of freedom to define which data they wish to obtain from the facility and to generate information in support of their learning programme.

This could be extended to many other areas of the curriculum, by looking at the real world science used across a range of industries.

Smith, 2006

These telepresence technologies are likely to develop over time and allow learners to experience, explore and interact with remote locations, often in foreign countries or environmentally sensitive places. The next step is to use immersive interfaces (virtual reality, haptics) to allow users to connect to and control cameras, robots and other devices remotely. These kinds of technologies already have military and medical applications, but as cost and complexity reduce, they could provide compelling learning experiences for all:

We may be on the verge of a new era, when the PC will get up off the desktop and allow us to see, hear, touch and manipulate objects in places where we are not physically present.

Gates, 2007

Context awareness

At the front-end of an AmI [ambient intelligence] system are a variety of tiny devices that can hear, see, or feel an end-user's presence. At the back-end, wireless-based networked systems make sense of these data, identifying the end-user and understanding his/her needs.

Raisinghani et al., 2004

As identification, location and sensing technologies come together in wirelessly connected networks linked to the

World Wide Web, our computer systems will be increasingly context aware. This means providing relevant information, in the right form, at the time and place it is needed. Context-aware systems should help filter the increasing amounts of information we have to deal with and make IT work for us. This would also allow learners to concentrate on the task rather than the technology.

Context aware computing is about a change from computer systems that need direct user input before carrying out a task to systems that can understand context and automatically and dynamically modify their behaviour. Ultimately this will mean systems that know who you are (your role, your preferences, previous actions), your location, what device you are using, what connectivity options and other services are available to you, your environment, what you are doing (are you in a meeting?) and possibly your emotional state and receptiveness to learning – affective computing. 'Affective computing' detects the emotional state and attention of the user through technologies such as voice analysis, gaze tracking, skin conductivity, facial expression analysis (machine vision) and user actions.

This should result in devices and software that intelligently adapt their behaviour based on a range of context related information, offering customised and personalised experiences: 'just in time' computing, which remains unobtrusive until needed. In ubiquitous computing the computer will have become embedded all around us in a variety of devices, objects and locations, for example MIT Project Oxygen (*http://www.oxygen.lcs.mit.edu/E21.html*) and EU MUSIC (*http://www.appearnetworks.com/EU-Research-Project-MUSIC.html*). This has been likened to the role of electricity and writing (Weiser and Brown, 1996) in our environment, both of which are fairly ubiquitous, but largely go unnoticed until needed.

Changing society, changing learners

In order to deliver engaging and meaningful education we need to understand our learners and what we are preparing them for.

Digital natives?

Twenty-first-century learners have never known a world without computers, instant communications and other digital technologies. Marc Prensky popularised the term 'digital natives' (Prensky, 2001a) to describe this generation, as opposed to the rest of us who are 'digital immigrants' and who despite adopting and using technology always retain 'an accent'. Prensky argues that this generation of learners are products of their digital, connected environment and experiences and therefore think and learn differently from previous generations. This follows the idea of neuroplasticity (Prensky, 2001b), whereby the brain adapts and reorganises itself from experience. The implication is that the current organisation of learning and its associated teaching methods do not necessarily meet the learning styles, preferences and expectations of today's students.

Many studies have shown the extent of young people's use of digital and connected technologies:

> the use of digital technology has been completely normalised by this generation, and it is now fully integrated into their daily lives.
>
> Hannon and Green, 2007

> For the 12–15 age groups, use of the internet is the most important technology in their lives – more important than television.
>
> DCSF, 2007

> As children age they begin to spend more time on the internet, and make heavier use of mobile phones. This is an important way in which the world has changed for all children and families in the last decade. These tools are now a popular part of older children's lives, and integral to the way in which many children learn about the world, and socialise with their friends.
>
> DCSF, 2007

However, some commentators have been too easily impressed by what they see young people doing with technology, possibly because they lack understanding and experience of the technologies themselves and how easy they can be to use. Although many young people are doing some sophisticated things with technology, this is not a generation of technical experts and much use of technology is superficial and about communicating and recreational activities with friends. What young people have are the characteristics young people have always had: no fear, plenty of spare time and strong cultural influences. So although many young people appear confident in their use of technology, this does not mean that they are all competent. Most possess neither in-depth technical knowledge nor the critical thinking skills needed to navigate the digital world effectively. Indeed a number of studies have recently rejected the 'digital native' idea and pointed to the lack of evidence to support it (e.g. Hannon and Green, 2007; Bennett, Maton and Kervin, 2008):

> The majority of young people simply use new media as tools to make their lives easier, strengthening their existing friendship networks rather than widening them. Almost all are now also involved in creative production, from uploading and editing photos to building and maintaining websites. However, we discovered a gap

between a smaller group of digital pioneers engaged in groundbreaking activities and the majority of children who rarely strayed into this category.

Hannon and Green, 2007

However, the way young people think about technology and its use may be different. As a recent worldwide survey of young people discovered, they do not see technology as a concept, and would not recognise many terms used in this chapter (Microsoft Advertising, n.d.). Only 16 per cent use terms like 'social networking'. For the others the technology is invisible, a natural part of their lives. This is not surprising. We do not see the things we grew up with as technology. The survey also picked up interesting cultural and sociological differences in the way technology was used in different countries, showing that society affects technology as much as technology society.

No doubt this generation has been influenced by digital technology and its effect on modern culture and society. This influence can be felt in the characteristics, behaviours and preferences of young people, which may present a challenge to educators to adapt to their needs and produce young people suited to the rapidly evolving world of work.

Net generation characteristics

Oblinger and Oblinger (2005) have described the apparent characteristics of this 'net generation' as:

- *Digital*. They have grown up with and are at ease with digital technologies; they favour visual displays over text.

- *Connected*. They use technology to keep in touch with their networks; they multitask and use multimodal communications.

- *Experiential.* They prefer to be engaged by learning by doing, rather than passive reading and listening; they also prefer to work on real things that matter.

- *Immediate.* They are used to and expect immediacy (instant messaging over e-mail).

- *Social.* They tend to prefer working in teams, empowered peer-to-peer learning, rather than instructor-led top-down approaches. They distinguish less between virtual and real world connections.

So this generation of learners has been shaped by society, culture and technology, as have we all. With an ageing population and an increased emphasis on life-long learning we need to consider all ages in our design of education and learning. Not surprisingly surveys (Dutton and Helsper, 2007; Ofcom, 2007; ONS, 2007) show that older people are less likely to use the internet, but even among the net generation there remains a digital divide. The reasons given for not using the internet are often to do with lack of knowledge and skills rather than lack of access *per se* (Dutton and Helsper, 2007).

Informal learning and digital literacy

Learners spend 80–90 per cent of their time not engaged in formal education. It is increasingly understood that the kind of learning that takes place outside institutions is not an extension of formal learning but a different type of learning and acquisition of skills and experience. This 'hidden curriculum' is already being enhanced by digital technologies:

> Increasingly individuals now have at their disposal the tools to be able to acquire, retrieve, capture and disseminate information for themselves through social

networks which they can help develop, organise and play an active role in. Outside formal education, individuals are becoming active creators and producers of knowledge and information. This represents a distinct cultural change in the way people work and collaborate and the tools they use for doing so.

Rudd, Colligan and Naik, 2006

Media and digital literacy (Buckingham, 2005; Jenkins, 2006) are key skills for learners to acquire for both formal and informal use of technology. Even Prensky notes that the digital natives may not be spending time on reflection, which is vital to good learning. Despite their facility with the web, the ability to appraise content critically and gauge its authenticity, credibility, bias (only 15 per cent of web pages link to an opposing view; Barabasi, 2002) and value is not something that comes naturally to the 'cut and paste' shortcut approaches of many learners. Indeed some recent papers (Bennet, Maton and Kervin, 2008; UCL, 2008; Hampton-Reeves et al., 2009; Head and Eisenberg, 2009; Melville, 2009) demonstrate quite clearly that the 'net generation' or 'digital natives' are not information literate in that they do not think critically about the information they find. They also need to be taught about risks (privacy, security, e-safety) and the legal and ethical issues associated with the internet. The new digital divide is not so much about inequality of access to hardware and connectivity, but around knowledge and skills:

We are witnessing an educational deficit between new media activity at home, in private, and that which takes place in formal educational and public environment... Educators and guardians need to ensure every young person, regardless of background and socio-economic position, can access the skills and knowledge to be full participants in the networked knowledge society. New media literacies should be social skills and part of a wider citizenship toolkit for a digital era.

Twist, 2007

New knowledge workers

The current generation of young people will reinvent the workplace, and the society they live in. They will do it along the progressive lines that are built into the technology they use everyday – of networks, collaboration, co-production and participation. The change in behaviour has already happened. We have to get used to it, accept that the flow of knowledge moves both ways and do our best to make sure that no one is left behind.

Hannon and Green, 2007

The workplace is increasingly valuing the types of softer, 21st-century skills that technology-enhanced learning can best deliver. In a globalised economy, it will be non-routine cognitive tasks that shape our competiveness, the ability to form teams, collaborate, find problems, analyse and apply information, think critically, communicate and be innovative and creative. It is less about applying knowledge to solve known problems.

As those in the net generation move into work, they will increasingly act as change agents and their expectations and preferences will influence the behaviour of forward-looking businesses. These new workers will insist on being able to customise their working structures, resources, tools and services. Workers are likely to change jobs more often, and be part of ad-hoc teams that come together for individual projects and then disperse. Our assumptions about how work is organised are likely to change. For example, location will become less important. Expertise location and being part of professional communities will be key to enabling flatter hierarchies and collaborative ways of working. Moreover, the need to keep learning new skills, reinventing oneself, should be supported by learners already having taken control of their education, learning to learn.

Consumerisation of IT

In the past, computer technology was expensive, complicated and business oriented. Therefore, technology adoption tended to start within business and public sector organisations and gradually filter into the homes of workers. However, we are now seeing a major reversal of this trend and many technology innovations are aimed at the consumer market and knowledgeable users are bringing their own technologies into the work space, as the corporate systems are not meeting their needs or expectations. Analysts have called this the consumerisation of IT (Gartner, 2005). As the cost, ease of use and availability of technologies has changed, users have become comfortable with and reliant on an increasing range of technologies in their personal lives. Indeed, much of the technology innovation and development now taking place, particularly around Web 2.0, is happening in the consumer space. Users are familiar with mobile devices, online communication and collaboration, media creation, computer games and a host of other technologies.

A classic example of the consumerisation trend has been the adoption of instant messaging (IM) by organisations. IM applications allow synchronous text chat between users as well as providing 'presence' information, such as informing a user when his or her contacts are online. These applications that now include features such as file sharing, voice communication and video conferencing have been immensely popular. Many people started installing these consumer grade applications on their work computers, usually without the consent of IT departments. IM enabled new ways of communicating and collaborating, with an immediacy not found with e-mail. However, being consumer applications there are serious security and auditing issues around their use. IT departments could either enforce a ban on their use (reducing productivity), turn a blind eye (leaving security issues) or embrace the technology and properly manage it. Now, corporate grade IM systems are common.

Consumersiation is underpinned by a number of trends:

- an increased range of affordable devices and (often free) services and content aimed at consumers, giving more freedom and choice

- technologies that are easier to use and consumers who are comfortable with a wide range of digital technologies in their lives

- users who have easy access to the means of digital production and distribution

- services and technologies that develop and change rapidly (perpetual beta)

- the increasing commoditisation of IT hardware

- users who are also shaping technology itself through new open approaches to development such as software being in perpetual beta, Web 2.0 open APIs, mashups and the power of the crowd

■ the blurring of boundaries between working, learning, playing and socialising, and users who expect to do all these activities on their devices.

So for education, more knowledgeable students with higher expectations are likely to demand greater use of digital technologies, and in the new education 'marketplace', institutions need to respond in order to compete.

Democratisation of technology

The consumerisation of IT has lowered the barriers to access, both to technology and to the means of media production and distribution. Inexpensive, easy to use technologies enable anyone to create professional looking text, video or audio and to publish it to the whole world via the internet. The media is no longer in the hands of the few, so we are moving from being a massive passive audience consuming content created by the few, to being an active audience of consumers and creators. This trend can be seen in the 'citizen journalist phenomenon', which has now become part of mainstream media. The 2007 Burma uprisings and the 2009 Iranian demonstrations reached the world via mobile digital technologies, and the internet and technology can help support democracy (Dutton, 2007). Users are also shaping technology itself through the new open approaches to development such as software being in perpetual beta, Web 2.0 open APIs and mashups, and the power of the crowd.

Autonomy vs control

Developments in technology and the behaviours and expectations of users present challenges to IT departments.

Traditionally, IT managers have tightly controlled and locked down the networks, applications and equipment made available to their users. This has been for very sound reasons: it helps ensure security and interoperability, and minimises management and support requirements, thus reducing costs. However, this approach now risks stifling innovation, handicapping increasingly technology savvy users and making IT systems irrelevant and unattractive. As businesses and learning institutions will need to compete for the digital natives who are their employees and students, the failure to change could make them uncompetitive with more agile organisations.

Users will expect to be able to select and customise their own tools and networks of information, and people. So there needs to be a new balance struck between freedom and control of IT systems. IT departments will need to provide robust, reliable base services, while leaving room for users to innovate and be more autonomous in their choice of technology. A one-size-fits-all offering will not be appropriate, although managed infrastructure, policies and guidelines will still be important. This kind of managed diversity will be helped by emerging technologies such as virtualisation. As the boundaries blur between working, learning, playing and socialising, so users will expect to do all these activities on their devices. Virtualisation will allow multiple, discrete environments to run on the same device, enabling secure separation of these different activities and avoiding substantial support overheads.

Conclusion

There are social, technical, ethical, political and security issues with all of the technologies discussed in this chapter. However, the need to adapt our education systems to take advantage of what technology can offer, meet the needs and expectations of our learners, and prepare them for the future cannot be ignored. This will no doubt result in changes to curricula and assessment so that we have a 21st-century system for 21st-century learners:

> Imagine a nation of horse riders with a clearly defined set of riding capabilities. In one short decade the motor car is invented and within that same decade many children become highly competent drivers extending the boundaries of their travel as well as developing entirely new leisure pursuits (like stock-car racing and hot rodding). At the end of the decade government ministers want to assess the true impact of automobiles on the nation's capability. They do it by putting everyone back on the horses and checking their dressage, jumping and trotting as before. Of course, we can all see that it is ridiculous.
>
> Heppell, 1994

The most talented students will still thrive in an instructor led, knowledge transmission heavy education system. But most learners need 'concrete, visualized, experiential, self-initiated, hands-on, and real-world learning opportunities' (Semenov, 2005). These are opportunities that digital, connected, social and pervasive technology can enable through allowing richer, context-based interactions backed up with teacher-led interpretation and reflection: 'The future is already here, it's just unevenly distributed' (Gibson, 2003).

References

Ambient Intelligence.org, website developed by Giuseppe Riva as part of the EU-funded VEPSY research project, *http://www.ambientintelligence.org/* (accessed 8 January 2010).

Anderson, P. (2007) *What is Web 2.0? Ideas, technologies and implications for education*. Bristol: Joint Information Systems Committee.

Arvind, D. K. and Wong, K. J. (2004) Speckled computing: disruptive technology for networked information appliances. In *Proceedings of the IEEE International Symposium on Consumer Electronics* (ISCE 2004), 219–223, *http://www.specknet.org/publications/Steven4_ICSE04.pdf* (accessed 8 January 2010).

Barabasi, A.-L. (2002) *Linked: the new science of networks*. Cambridge, MA: Perseus.

BBC News (2007) Web 2.0 'neglecting good design', 14 May, *http://news.bbc.co.uk/1/hi/technology/6653119.stm* (accessed 7 January 2010).

Becta (2006a) *The Becta Review 2006*. Coventry: Becta.

Becta (2006b) *Web 2.0: what might it mean for developers*. Coventry: Becta.

Becta (2007) *Harnessing Technology Schools Survey*. Coventry: Becta.

Becta (2008) Web 2.0 technologies for learning at KS3 and KS4 – project overview, *http://partners.becta.org.uk/index.php?section=rh&catcode=_re_rp_02&rid=14543* (accessed 5 February 2010).

Benford, S. (2005) *Future Location Based Experiences*. Bristol: Joint Information Systems Committee.

Bennett, S., Maton, K. and Kervin, L. (2008) The 'digital natives' debate: a critical review of the evidence, *British Journal of Educational Technology*, 39 (5), 775–86.

Bruner, J. (1969) *The Process of Education*. Cambridge, MA: Harvard University Press.

Bryant, L. (2007) Emerging trends in social software for education. In Becta, *Emerging Technologies for Learning*, vol. 2. Coventry: Becta.

Buckingham, D. (2005) *The Media Literacy of Children and Young People: a review of the literature*. London: Centre for the Study of Children Youth and Media, Institute of Education.

Campbell, A. (2005) RFID in museums: another growing market, RFID weblog, 22 August, *http://www.rfid-weblog.com/50226711/rfid_in_museums_another_growing_market.php* (accessed 7 January 2010).

CETIS (2005) The personal learning environments blog, Centre for Educational Technology Interoperability Standards, Joint

Information Systems Committee, *http://www.cetis.ac.uk/members/ ple/resources/ple_summary* (accessed 7 January 2010).

Crook, C. and Harrison, C. (2008) *Web 2.0 Technologies for Learning at Key Stages 3 and 4: summary report.* Coventry: Becta.

DCSF (2007) *Children and Young People Today: evidence to support the development of the Children's Plan.* London: Department for Children, Schools and Families.

Downes, S. (2007) *Learning Networks in Practice.* In Becta, *Emerging Technologies for Learning*, vol. 2. Coventry: Becta.

Dutton, W. H. (2007) Through the network (of networks) – the fifth estate, prepared for an inaugural lecture. Oxford Internet Institute, University of Oxford, 15 October.

Dutton, W. H. and Helsper, E. J. (2007) *The Internet in Britain.* Oxford: Oxford Internet Institute.

Franklin, T. and van Harmelen, M. (2007) *Web 2.0 for Content for Learning and Teaching in Higher Education.* Bristol: Joint Information Systems Committee.

Fujimura, N. and Doi, M. (2006) Collecting students' degree of comprehension with mobile phones, *http://delivery.acm.org/ 10.1145/1190000/1181244/p123-fujimura.pdf?key1= 1181244&key2=6214984611&coll=ACM&dl=ACM&CFID= 15151515&CFTOKEN=6184618* (accessed 7 January 2010).

Gartner (2005) Gartner says consumerization will be most significant trend affecting IT during next 10 years, Gartner press release, *http://www.gartner.com/press_releases/asset_138285_11 .html* (accessed 7 January 2010).

Gates, B. (2007) A robot in every home, *Scientific American*, January.

Gibson, W. (2003) Books of the year 2003, *The Economist*, 4 December, *http://www.economist.com/books/displaystory.cfm? story_id=E1_NNGVRJV* (accessed 6 August 2007).

Gilbert, C. (2006) *2020 Vision: report of the Teaching and Learning in 2020 Review Group.* London: Department for Education and Science.

Hamblen, M. (2007) Berners-Lee urges vendors to keep mobile internet open, *Computerworld*, 14 November, *http://www .computerworld.com/s/article/9046899/Berners_Lee_urges_ vendors_to_keep_mobile_Internet_open* (accessed 5 February 2010).

Hampton-Reeves, S., Mashiter, C., Westaway, J., Lumsden, P., Day, H., Hewertson, H. and Hart, A. (2009) *Students' Use of Research Content in Teaching and Learning*, report for the Joint Information Systems Committee (JISC), *http://ie-repository .jisc.ac.uk/407/1/Students_Use_of_Research_Content.pdf* (accessed 15 January 2010).

Hannon, C. and Green, H. (2007) *Their Space: education for a digital generation*. London: Demos.

Head, A. J. and Eisenberg, M. B. (2009) *Finding Context: what today's college students say about conducting research in the digital age*, Project Information Literacy progress report, *http:// www.projectinfolit.org/pdfs/PIL_ProgressReport_2_2009.pdf* (accessed 15 January 2010).

Heppell, S. (1994) Multimedia and learning: normal children, normal lives and real change. In J. Underwood (ed.) *Computer-based Learning: potential into practice*. London: David Fulton.

In Stat (2006) MEMS in mobile handsets will top $1 billion by 2010, *http://www.instat.com/newmk.asp?ID=1671&SourceID= 00000366000000000000* (accessed 8 January 2010).

Institute for the Future (2006) *Map of Future Forces Affecting Education*. Cincinnati, OH: KnowledgeWorks Foundation.

ITU (2005) *The Internet of Things*, ITU Internet Report. Geneva: International Telecommunications Union.

Jenkins, H. (2006) *The Challenges of Participatory Culture Media Education for the 21st Century*. Chicago, IL: MacArthur Foundation.

Leadbeater, C. (2005) *The Shape of Things to Come: personalised learning through collaboration*. London: Department for Education and Science.

Lenhart, A. and Madden, M. (2005) *Teen Content Creators and Consumers*. Washington, DC: Pew Internet and American Life Project, *http://www.pewinternet.org/Reports/2005/Teen-Content-Creators-and-Consumers.aspx* (accessed 8 January 2010).

Ley, D. (2007) Ubiquitous computing. In Becta, *Emerging Technologies for Learning*, vol. 2. Coventry: Becta.

Livingstone, S. and Bober, M. (2005) *UK Children Go Online: final report of key project findings*. London: London School of Economics, *http://www.citizensonline.org.uk/site/media/documents/ 1521_UKCGO-final-report.pdf* (accessed 8 January 2010).

Melville, D. (2009) *Higher Education in a Web 2.0 World: report of the independent committee of inquiry into the impact on higher education of students' widespread use of Web 2.0 technologies*, *http://www.jisc.ac.uk/media/documents/publications/heweb20rptv1.pdf* (accessed 15 January 2010).

Microsoft Advertising (n.d.) *Young Adults Revealed: the lives and motivations of 21st century youth*, *http://advertising.microsoft.com/norge/WWDocs/User/no-no/ResearchLibrary/Research Report/Young_Adults_booklet.pdf* (accessed 5 February 2010).

Naismith, L., Lonsdale, P., Vavoula, G. and Sharples, M. (2004) *Literature Review in Mobile Technologies and Learning*. Bristol: Futurelab.

NeoMedia (2009) BBC/HP – The Coast Mobile Experience, *http://www.neom.com/casestudy-5.php* (accessed 5 February 2010).

New Media Consortium and Educause Learning Initiative (2006) *The Horizon Report*. Austin, TX: New Media Consortium.

Nussbaum, E. (2007) Say everything. Kids the internet and the end of privacy: the greatest generation gap since rock and roll, *New York Magazine*, *http://nymag.com/news/features/27341/* (accessed 7 January 2010).

Oblinger, D. and Oblinger, J. (2005) Is it age or IT: first steps toward understanding the net generation. In D. Oblinger and J. Oblinger (eds) *Educating the Net Generation*. Boulder, CO: Educause.

Ofcom (2007) *The Communications Market Report*. London: Ofcom.

ONS (2007) *Focus on the Digital Age*. Newport: Office of National Statistics.

Owen, M., Grant, L., Sayers, S. and Facer, K. (2006) *Social Software and Learning*. Bristol: Futurelab.

Pachler, N. (ed.) (2007) *Mobile Learning: towards a research agenda*. London: WLE Centre, Institute of Education.

Papert, S. (1980) *Mindstorms: children, computers, and powerful ideas*. Hassocks: Harvester Press.

Prensky, M. (2001a) Digital natives, digital immigrants, *On the Horizon*, 9 (5).

Prensky, M. (2001b) Do they really *think* differently?, *On the Horizon*, 9 (6).

Raisinghani, M. S., Benoit, A., Ding, J., Gomez, M., Gupta, K., Gusila, V., Power, D. and Schmedding, O. (2004) Ambient intelligence: changing forms of human-computer interaction and their social implications, *Journal of Digital Information*, 5 (4).

Roush, W. (2005) Social machines: computing means connecting, *MIT Technology Review*, August.

Rudd, T., Colligan, F. and Naik, R. (2006) *Learner Voice*. Bristol: Futurelab.

Rundle, M. and Conley, C. (2007) *Ethical Implications of EmergingTechnologies: a survey*. Paris: Unesco.

Sefton-Green, J. (2004) *Literature Review in Informal Learning with Technology Outside School*. Bristol: Futurelab.

Seidensticker, B. (2006) *Future Hype: the myths of technology change*. San Francisco, CA: Berrett-Koehler.

Semenov, A. (2005) *ICT in Schools*. Paris: Unesco.

Sharples, M., Taylor, J. and Vavoula, G. (2005) Towards a theory of mobile learning, *http://www.mlearn.org.za/CD/papers/Sharples-%20Theory%20of%20Mobile.pdf* (accessed 7 January 2010).

Sharples, M., Taylor, J. and Vavoula, G. (2007) A theory of learning for the mobile age. In R. Andrews and C. Haythornthwaite (eds) *The Sage Handbook of E-learning Research*. London: Sage.

Shirky, C. (2003) The semantic web, syllogism and world view, *http://www.shirky.com/writings/semantic_syllogism.html* (accessed 7 January 2010).

Smith, P. (2006) *An evaluation of the Bradford Robotic Telescope*, Hoshin, *http://www.telescope.org/articles/YFRobotics.pdf* (accessed 7 January 2010).

Socrates (470 BC) *Phaedrus*.

Squidoo (n.d.) A guide to declarative living, *http://www.squidoo.com/declare/* (accessed 7 January 2010).

Stead, G. (2006) Mobile technologies: transforming the future of learning. In Becta, *Emerging Technologies for Learning*, vol. 2. Coventry: Becta.

Twining, P. (2007) *The Schome-NAGTY Teen Second Life Pilot Final Report*. Milton Keynes: Open University.

Twist, J., (2007) The challenge of new digital literacies and the hidden curriculum. In Becta, *Emerging Technologies for Learning*, vol. 2. Coventry: Becta.

UCL (2008) *Information Behaviour of the Researcher of the Future: a CIBER briefing paper*, executive summary, University College London, *http://www.ucl.ac.uk/slais/research/ciber/downloads/ ggexecutive.pdf* (accessed 19 March 2008).

Vygotsky, L. S. (1978) *Mind and Society: the development of higher mental processes*, translation. Cambridge, MA: Harvard University Press.

Wal, T. V. (2009) Personal InfoCloud, *http://personalinfocloud .com/* (accessed 7 January 2010).

Ward, M., Van Kranenburg, R. and Backhouse, G. (2006) RFID: frequency, standards, adoption and innovation, JISC Technology and Standards Watch, *http://www.rfidconsultation .eu/docs/ficheiros/TSW0602.pdf* (accessed 7 January 2010).

Weinberger, D. (2002a) *Small Pieces Loosely Joined: a unified theory of the web.* Jackson, TN: Perseus Books Group.

Weinberger, D. (2002b) The semantic argument web, *http://www .hyperorg.com/backissues/joho-jun26-02.html#semantic* (accessed 7 January 2010).

Weiser, M. (1991) The computer for the 21st century, *Scientific American*, February, *http://www.ics.uci.edu/~dutt/ics212- wq05/weiser-sci-am-sep-91.pdf* (accessed 7 January 2010).

Weiser, M. and Brown, J. S. (1996) *The Coming of Age of Calm Technology.* Palo Alto, CA: Xerox PARC.

Wijngaards, G., de Jong, J. and van Rooijen, O. (2007) *Profile Sites: a survey of young people and social networking sites.* Rotterdam: INHOLLAND School of Communication & Media.

Part 4:
Conclusion

7

Meeting the challenge

Liz Hart

Introduction

This chapter will provide a brief overview of the technological changes and developments that have enabled Web 2.0 to happen and, more importantly, some of the individual and social changes that have come about as a result. The general impact of Web 2.0 will be evaluated mainly in the context of the role of libraries and the information professional.

There is frequently little agreement about what Web 2.0 constitutes even though it has been around for five years. Arguably, the most definitive paper appeared in 2005 from Tim O'Reilly (2005). In 'What is Web 2.0?' he postulates commencement of Web 2.0 from the bursting of the dot.com bubble in 2001. In a conference brainstorming session in 2003 it was concluded that the web was still vital and at some kind of 'turning point', which justified the adopting of the Web 2.0 term. By default, and rather unsurprisingly, this has tended to mean that what came before Web 2.0 is referred to at Web 1.0.

Change and connectivity

Web 2.0 is a process where technological change is allowing new ways of dynamic interaction and participation. Like most changes this is having a gradual but significant, and frequently highly visible, impact. This process of change is powered by three main factors:

- Computer power is growing exponentially.

- The technology is becoming embedded into the everyday life of citizens in the developed world.

- Most significantly, there is connectivity providing a new, flexible and dynamic way to link all the bits and pieces of the web together.

Bill Sharpe has summarised the change in a chapter on the ambient web in Becta's *Emerging Technologies for Learning*:

> Rough calculations of the computing power that has been shipped by the chip makers suggests that the thing we call 'computers' represent no more than 1 per cent of the computing that is going on around us. The other 99 per cent is hard at work controlling cars, central heating, doors, kiosks, telecommunications and utility networks and most of the things we rely on. What is happening now is that the relentless progress in both power and density is combining with the big third factor – connectivity.
>
> Sharpe, 2006

This connectivity enables the web to become a platform for activity of all kinds. O'Reilly has produced a meme map, which attempts, quite successfully, to visualise Web 2.0 and many of the impacts and opportunities connect to the concept (Figure 7.1).

This map offers not only a summary of some of the ideas and concepts within Web 2.0 but also clearly shows some of the opportunities and challenges. It is not easy for anyone

Figure 7.1 Web 2.0 meme map

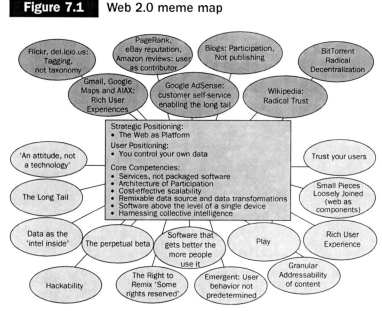

Source: O'Reilly (2005), reproduced with permission

used to the Web 1.0 environment to consider the idea of software in a state of constant beta, which improves the more people use it and the more it 'learns' from that usage. The idea of users employing their own free text tagging in services such as Flickr or Delicious rather than any predetermined taxonomy could be regarded as a threat, but is clearly also an opportunity for the information professional. In fact, subsequent to the development of the concept of Web 2.0, there has developed the term Library 2.0. A good explanation of this can be found in an article by those credited with being the first to use the term, Michael Casey, and Laura Savastinuk (Casey and Savastinuk, 2006). Wikipedia defined Library 2.0 in this way:

> Library 2.0 is a loosely defined model for a modernised form of library service that reflects a transition within

the library world in the way that services are delivered to users... With Library 2.0 library services are constantly updated and re-evaluated to best service library users. Library 2.0 also attempts to harness the library user in the design and the implementation of library services by encouraging feedback and participation.

Wikipedia, 2008

It is important that the technological developments that have enabled these opportunities to occur are clearly recognised, if only to perceive and understand what might be coming next. What are the key differences between Web 2.0 and what went before (the so called Web 1.0)? The major difference lies in the concept of what is delivered. In Web 1.0 are the products and companies such as Microsoft and Oracle, which produce reliable and recognisable software with specific licensing, sales and release schedules. Products provided by the Web 2.0 companies do not follow this pattern and are in essence a form of service. They grow and develop through a process of continuous improvement and customers pay either directly or indirectly for the service provided. The customers also become an integral part of the development cycle and success. As O'Reilly summarises: 'There is an implicit "architecture of participation", a built in ethic of cooperation, in which the services acts primarily as the intelligent broker, connecting the edges to each other and harnessing the power of the users themselves' (Sharpe, 2006).

The power of the user

The idea of harnessing the power of users is critical to an understanding of Web 2.0. For the first time people can establish their own individual, personal data and information and, if they choose, make it available to others. This has created what has been referred to by Henry Jenkins, Director of the Comparative Media Studies Program at the Massachusetts Institute of Technology, as a 'participatory culture' (Jenkins, 2006), of which more later in this chapter. Much of the power of the web is based around the ability to hyperlink, essentially because this enables the information discovery process to be not only individualised but also actively offered to others as a potential route for their own use.

Some companies actively exploit this user activity to produce a better 'product'. Amazon is a good example of this: it actively seeks user input, reviews and comment, which adds value to the 'product' and also establishes a sense of ownership and participation to exist for their customers. Amazon also uses customer search activity to produce better and more helpful results, for example, by always leading with those that are the 'most popular'. This technique also personalises the data and information – an approach which is essential to the understanding of Web 2.0. Once this personalisation, sense of ownership and dynamic participate are understood, it is relatively straightforward to understand why folksonomies such as Delicious and Flickr have emerged so rapidly.

Folksonomies are entirely based on users (participants) providing information and data and then categorising that information. Users (or participants) employ freely chosen terms, which are flexible and not preordained. Although the challenges of such an approach are obvious to an information professional, so are the advantages and opportunities. The user is generating how information and resources are retrieved – or indeed how they are lost! This could be regarded as an information revolution in the true sense of the word. Flickr tags allow searchers to find images concerning a certain topic such as a place name or subject matter. The service was also an early adopter of tag clouds, which provide access to images tagged with the most popular keywords. In addition users are encouraged to organise their images into sets or groups that fall under the same heading. However, sets are more flexible than more traditional methods as they can belong to one set, many sets or none at all. These sets represent a form of categorical metadata rather than a physical hierarchy. There is also considerable potential to achieve semantic as well as the subject or term categorisation of information. The service also reflects, perhaps more appropriately, how 'ordinary people' retrieve information for themselves. This naturally leads to multiple retrieval opportunities and also potentially that similar information may not necessarily be as 'connected' as it might be... but surely this is where information professionals can play a key role?

Trust and do it yourself

Unsurprisingly these developments have gained the name 'do it yourself' technologies. Probably the best know of these is Wikipedia. Significantly, in the context of Web 2.0, the word wiki means 'quick' in Hawaiian. Wikis are websites that allow users or participants to add, edit and delete content. They were originally conceived to allow a group of participants, such as those involved in a research project, to work collaboratively and dynamically together. However, Wikipedia goes one step further as an online encyclopaedia, which allows any registered user to contribute. It is therefore compiled, edited and re-edited by 'people', and although there is an element of moderation, it essentially relies on good will, trust and peer assessment and evaluation.

The 'trust' elements of this are new and radical, the technology something of a sideline. If you consider the meme map produced by O'Reilly (2005) (Figure 7.1), this brings the description of Web 2.0 as 'an attitude not a technology' to life. This is an idea echoed by Stephen Fry (author and broadcaster) who is quoted by Wikipedia as indicating that in his view Web 2.0 is:

> an idea in people's heads rather than reality. It's actually an idea that the reciprocity between the user and the provider is what's emphasised. In other words genuine interactivity if you like simply because people can upload as well as download.

Whether real or not, the advantages and dynamic applicability of such a participatory product are clear. Wikipedia pre-eminently recognises that information does change and that 'facts' alter with new discoveries. The content of such a product is not fixed and is always open to challenge and change. The opportunities for error, for misinformation, exist, but so does the need for information professionals to proactively participate. Finally it is significant that Wikipedia is now formally acknowledged as one of the most popular websites in the world.

This argument that Web 2.0 is not real has been echoed by some technical experts. Tim Berners Lee has questioned whether we can use the term in any meaningful way since many of the technological components of Web 2.0 have existed since the early days of the web (Wikipedia, 2010). However, the key to Web 2.0 is participation and use of those tools.

Synthesis

How does all this information link together on the web? The ubiquitous technology that underpins much of the web is

Really Simple Syndication (RSS). Essentially this is used to syndicate news and website content across the web by making it machine readable. Users who subscribe to an RSS enabled website can have content 'pushed' to them automatically via RSS aggregators or news readers. The most obvious and practical applications of this technology are already widely in use for educational purposes, for current financial information, for weather or for tourism. This 'push' technology is another key element of Web 2.0 and again it depends on dynamic user participation. Users not only link to the website personally but are then dynamically notified on each occasion the web page changes. Skrenta (2005) has called this the 'incremental web'. A parallel development is the use of permalinks – an apparently trivial piece of technology, which permits the establishment of a permanent link to a sentence, paragraph or word within a web page. The permanent link that is established to the item allows you to add your own comments, and discussion, argument and 'chat' emerge. These technologies have come to be commonly referred to by some as 'web feed' technologies.

This represents the real power of participatory communities, which are beginning to have a huge social, economic and business impact. In *Wikinomics* (2006), Don Tapscott and Anthony D. Williams show how masses of people can participate in the economy and the potential impacts of this global collaboration for businesses and the global economy. In their view collaboration changes everything and by 'people' acting together what will result is what they refer to as 'economic democracy'. Companies are all planning how they will exploit, market and compete in this new business environment. One of the key areas is integrated communications where existing e-mail, mobile phone and Voice over Internet Protocol (VOIP) will be combined. Significantly, Microsoft has already launched a strategy for unified communications, which will concentrate on streamlining and simplifying communication tools and enhancing dynamic collaboration, particularly for business.

The smart web

Essentially the new Web 2.0 communication tools have the capability to 'learn' about people. This obviously has serious ethical issues, which will need to be appropriately and firmly addressed, but if properly managed it also has huge opportunities. From an information professional's perspective, information can be selectively 'pushed' to users based on context and location, matching the user's immediate needs and interests just at the right time. This 'just in time' approach to the provision of information contracts with the traditional 'just in case' paradigm represented by most libraries. The power to profile users will enable retrieval capability from all available digital environments to be selectively maximised and the information dynamic delivered through mobile devices, PCs or portals – all based on personalised and individual (and by assumption different) needs. For perhaps the first time, there may be answers to the questions: 'Who are your users?' and 'How do they behave in the digital environment?'. As a result of such developments information professionals can be some of the leaders in the proactive provision of information.

Delivery and provision of information is enabled to change but it will not be possible to exploit such situations without a shift in attitude, approach and perhaps also skills. The MacArthur Foundation has launched a five-year digital and learning initiative to help determine how digital technologies are changing the way young people learn, play, socialise and participate in civic life. In an occasional paper that has emerged from this initiative 11 new skills and literacies have been established, including:

- *performance*: the ability to adopt alternative identities for the purpose of improvisation and discovery

- *appropriation*: the ability to meaningfully sample and remix media content

- *collective intelligence*: the ability to pool knowledge and compare notes with others towards a common goal

- *judgement*: the ability to evaluate the reliability and credibility of different information sources

- *networking*: the ability to search for, synthesise and disseminate information (Jenkins, 2006).

Skills full circle

Jenkins' argument is that 'textual literacy remains a central skill in the 21st century' and that in this context the traditional research skills 'assume an even greater importance as students venture beyond collections that have been screened by librarians to the more open space of the web'. These conclusions complement a similar theme in a work by David F. Warlick, which examines a redefinition of literacy (Warlick, 2007). Warlick's premise is that as technology becomes more and more embedded and an integral part of daily life it will be necessary fundamentally to reconsider what is meant by literacy. His view is that 'if our children learn to read they will not be literate'. Jenkins also recognises real and substantial challenges in what he refers to as the participation gap: the transparency problem and the 'ethics challenge'.

The term 'participation gap' has been used for some time to describe the unequal access to opportunities, skills and knowledge experienced by young people in preparation for participating in the world of tomorrow. Although Jenkins uses it in relation to young people, there is also a participation gap among the poor and the elderly. Jenkins uses 'transparency problem' to describe the challenge for young people in seeing clearly the ways in which media shape perceptions of the world. Finally, he uses 'ethics challenge' to explain the breakdown of the traditional ways young people are prepared for public roles.

Concluding remarks

All these are challenges, not just for the young, and they are all areas where an information professional can and does make a difference by the active application of professional skills and knowledge. Libraries from all sectors are making a difference with the support and training in information literacy. Public and academic libraries in particular see this as one of their key services and thereby tacitly acknowledge that without such skills their users potentially face disenfranchisement.

In a CILIP conference keynote speech, Lynne Brindley outlined the essential need for a change of approach and attitude in the information age. Her argument was that as people in the developed world freely create information and digital data of all kinds, the web can be overwhelming: 'We are both dis-intermediated and needed as never before' (Brindley, 2007).

We can see that the information and learning landscape is changing rapidly (chapters 1 and 2). What is clear is that, even if with small steps, the library community needs to grasp firmly the varied and myriad opportunities and developments that are currently on offer, some of which have been described above (chapters 5 and 6). There is a good case for adopting

Web 2.0 technologies both to train ourselves (Chapter 4) and to facilitate learning in others (Chapter 3). The alternative is potential extinction or the appropriation of information skills by other professional areas. In such a context, trying small incremental implementations, which improve on existing services in new and more proactive ways, is a potential way forward. As Brindley said: 'Act smart and just do it.'

References

Brindley, L. (2007) Risk, relevance and roles in the information age, keynote speech at CILIP Umbrella conference.

Casey, M. and Savastinuk, L. (2006) Library 2.0: service for the next generation library, *Library Journal*, 1 September, *http:// www.libraryjournal.com/article/CA6365200.html* (accessed 7 January 2010).

Jenkins, H. (2006) *Confronting the Challenges of Participatory Culture: media education for the 21st century.* Chicago, IL: MacArthur Foundation, *http://digitallearning.macfound.org/atf/ cf/%7B7E45C7E0-A3E0-4B89-AC9C-E807E1B0AE4E% 7D/JENKINS_WHITE_PAPER.PDF* (accessed 7 January 2010).

O'Reilly, T. (2005) What is Web 2.0?: design patterns and business models for the next generation of software, *http://oreilly.com/ web2/archive/what-is-web-20.html* (accessed 7 January 2010).

Sharpe, B. (2006) The ambient web. In Becta, *Emerging Technologies for Learning*, vol. 1. Coventry: Becta.

Skrenta, R. (2005) The incremental web, 12 February, *http://blog .topix.com/archives/000066.html*, (accessed 18 January 2010).

Tapscott, D. and Williams, A. D. (2006) *Wikinomics: how mass collaboration changes everything.* London: Atlantic Books.

Warlick, D. F. (2007) *Redefining Literacy for the 21st Century.* Santa Barbara, CA: Linworth.

Wikipedia (2008) Library 2.0, *http://en.wikipedia.org/wiki/ Library_2.0* (accessed 7 January 2010).

Wikipedia (2010) Web 2.0, *http://en.wikipedia.org/wiki/Web_2.0* (accessed 22 February 2010).

Index

Breinigsville, PA USA
03 May 2010
237190BV00003B/2/P